Sunset

GREENHOUSES

BY FIONA GILSENAN AND THE EDITORS OF SUNSET BOOKS

SUNSET BOOKS · MENLO PARK, CALIFORNIA

GROWING GREEN

As their confidence and knowledge increase, many gardeners eventually develop an interest in starting or propagating their own plants. Others become fascinated with a particular type of plant, perhaps orchids or exotic tropicals, and want to start a collection. Still others simply wish to bring their love of the outdoors into the house—to have a great place to sit with the Sunday paper, surrounded by their favorite plants. No matter what the motivation, the result is the same: It's time to think about a greenhouse or conservatory.

But that is only the beginning. Developments in glazing materials, improvements in structural design, and a new interest in conservatory gardening have led to a broader range of choices than

ever for the greenhouse consumer. In these pages you'll find a comprehensive overview of the types of structures available, and a practical guide to constructing one.

Remember above all that a greenhouse is a place where you can work true plant magic; increasing your horticultural knowledge and persuading your flowers and vegetables to grow like never before. In the process, you'll experience a wealth of pleasures and rewards.

For their assistance in preparing this book we gratefully acknowledge the following people: Ellen Wells, Janice Hale and the Hobby Greenhouse Association, Greg Header of Solar Innovations, and Carol and Charley Yaw of Charley's Greenhouse Supply.

SUNSET BOOKS

Vice President, General Manager: Richard A. Smeby

Vice President, Editorial Director: Bob Doyle

Production Director: Lory Day

Art Director: Vasken Guiragossian

Staff for this book:

Managing Editor: Fiona Gilsenan

Sunset Books Senior Editor, Gardening: Marianne Lipanovich

Copy Editors: Gail E. Nelson, Elissa Rabellino

Proofreader: Lura Dymond

Indexer: Erin Hartshorn

Photo Researchers: Melinda Anderson, Kathleen Olson

Production Coordinator: Patricia S. Williams

Assistant Editors: Bridget Biscotti Bradley, Susan M. Guthrie

Contributing Writers: Janice L. Hale, Ellen C. Wells

Essayists: Charles E. Dills, Debbie Ellis, judywhite, Libby Rich

Consultants: Carol Yaw, Charley Yaw

Art Director: Alice Rogers

Illustrators: Erin O'Toole, Mark Pechenik

Computer Production: Linda Bouchard, Susan Bryant Caron

Cover: Photography by Phil Harvey. Photo styling by Melinda Anderson. Border photography by Fiona Gilsenan

PHOTOGRAPHERS:

Christine Alicino: 34 right; **Greg Allikas:** 67 top; **Scott Atkinson:** 61 center; **Max E. Badgley:** 91 left; **Patricia J. Bruno/Positive Images:** 25; **Ralph Byther:** 86 top, 89 left, center left; **Charley's Greenhouse Supply:** 32, 35, 39 top, bottom, 41 bottom, 42 bottom, 43, 65 top left, center, 76; **Peter Christiansen:** 55; **Candace Cochrane/Positive Images:** 9 bottom, 12 top; **Sir Terence Conran:** 27 right; **Crandall and Crandall:** 72 top, 86 center top, bottom, 91 center right; **Alan and Linda Detrick:** 91 bottom center; **Thomas Eltzroth:** 89 center right; **Mark Englund/Juliana Greenhouses:** 15 bottom left; **Farm Wholesale:** 29 bottom; **Derek Fell:** 3 bottom right, 11 top, 58; **Fiona Gilsenan:** 30 all, 74, 75, 81, 86 center bottom, 88 bottom left, bottom right; **John Glover:** 27 top left, 34 left, 44, 49 all, 80 top, back cover right; **Ken Gutmaker:** 54 left; **Jerry Harpur:** 14 bottom, 56; **Lynne Harrison:** 8 bottom; **Hartley Botanic, Ltd. (UK) for Private Garden Greenhouse Systems (USA):** 53; **Greg Header/Solar Innovations:** 3 bottom left, 52, 92; **Saxon Holt/PhotoBotanic:** 68, 77; **Horticultural Photography:** 23; **James Frederick Housel:** 54 right; **Jerry Howard/Positive Images:** 50 bottom, 60 bottom, 73, 82, 83 top; **Interior Archives/Beddow:** 51 bottom left; **Interior Archives/Pilkington:** 51 top, back cover bottom left; **judywhite:** 2, 6 bottom, 9 top right, 40, 67 bottom; **Juliana Greenhouses:** 19; **Lee Valley Tools Ltd.:** 83 bottom; **Lynn Karlin:** 7 right; **Jim McCausland:** 3 top right, 16, 63, 78; **Mioulane/M.A.P.:** 72 bottom; **Oak Leaf Conservatories Ltd.:** 3 center, 46; **Marie O'Hara:** 13 bottom; **Hugh Palmer:** 48 top, bottom, 51, right; **Pamela K. Peirce:** 91 center left; **Norm Plate:** 11 bottom left, 61 left, right, 62, 64, 65 bottom, 84, 85; **Harry Smith Collection:** 3 top left, 4, 7 top left, bottom left, 8 top, 9 top left, 11 bottom right, 13, top, 28, 29 top, 42 left, 80 bottom, back cover top left; **Solar Innovations:** 1; **Southern Living Magazine/Sylvia Martin:** 22; **Southern Living Magazine/Van Chaplin:** 50 top; **J. G. Strauch, Jr.:** 89 right; **Derek St. Romaine:** 6 top, 10, 26 top, bottom, 38, 88 top; **Texas Greenhouse:** 18, 41 top; **Weber/Visuals Unlimited:** 88 bottom center; **Ron West:** 91 right; **Jennifer Wheatley/GardenPhotos.com:** 66; **Elizabeth Whiting & Associates:** 12 bottom, 14 top, 15 right.

The editors would also like to thank the following: Tom Alexander, Steve Bender, Rebecca Dye, Keri Lahl, Monty Lucas, Terry Martin (AIA), Jane McCreary, Lee Payne, Marie Peterson, Tamara Pugh, Frank Ricigliano, Helene Robertson, Santa Barbara Greenhouse Co., Linda Selden, Larry L. Smith, Shane Smith, Sue Sullivan, Britta Swartz, and Thompson & Morgan.

CONTENTS

GARDENING UNDER GLASS 5

A Matter of Style • A World Apart • Attached to the House • Tucked Away • Inside View

BUILDING BASICS 17

Be Your Own Builder • Proper Placement • Growing Greenhouses • A Solid Foundation • Flooring • Framing Options • Doors and Windows • You Need to Vent • Powering the Greenhouse • Maintaining Warmth • Let There Be Light • Water, Water • Interior Details

GARDEN ROOMS 47

Conservatory or Greenhouse? • Sun Spaces • Building Considerations • Interior Water Features • Conservatory Plants

INDOOR GROWING GUIDE 59

Growing Under Glass • A Year Indoors • Equipment and Supplies • In Pursuit of Orchids • From Tiny Seeds • A Cut Above • My Bromeliads • The Great Outdoors • Using Cold Frames • Greenhouse Beds • Hydroponics • Growing Cactus and Succulents • Troubleshooting

GREENHOUSE PROJECTS 93

Portable PVC • Solar Pit • Wood Gable • Aluminum-Frame Kit • Lightweight Lean-To • Garden Shed • Spacious Stand-Alone • A Custom Job

RESOURCE GUIDE 110
INDEX 112

The practice of gardening under glass has evolved very far from its straightforward origins. No longer is a greenhouse merely a glazed structure designed to extend the growing season. Instead, the

GARDENING UNDER
GLASS

term has come to mean anything from a simple wooden structure in which seeds are started and winter vegetables stored, to the most elaborate conservatories, fully climate-controlled and designed to house tropical fruits, exotic flowers, or extensive specialty plant collections. So whether you are a hobby gardener with a typical suburban lot or a homeowner seeking to expand your indoor living space, the following pages will give you an idea of the range of options available. Due to the rising popularity of true conservatories, American gardeners can now find a fine selection of mail-order and custom-made greenhouse options. And if you're a do-it-yourself builder, the structures shown in this chapter are sure to spark your imagination and get you started on the design process.

Even a modest-size greenhouse and cold frame can provide plenty of seedlings to fill an average-size garden with flowers and vegetables. It doesn't take long for the tiny plants in the garden to fill in.

A MATTER
OF STYLE

Simply because a greenhouse is a functional building doesn't mean it has to look utilitarian.

The only hard-and-fast design rule for any garden structure is that it should either complement or blend into the surrounding architecture and the style of the garden. Beyond that, you can feel free to let your imagination—and even your budget—run wild. A greenhouse can become a focal point of the garden, an extension to your home, a backyard retreat, or even a 'folly'—an architectural extravagance built purposefully to please the eye.

This thoroughly modern display greenhouse in France is based on a teepee design. Poles of sturdy bamboo form the basic structural members and heavy plastic film provides a lightweight glazing material. More fanciful than functional, it could nevertheless inspire you to create a seasonal model for your home garden. Peas, beans, tomatoes, and leafy greens would benefit from the additional warmth and protection from the elements.

One of America's finest public greenhouses is at Wave Hill on the grounds of a former estate in the Bronx, New York. Like other large-scale botanical greenhouses, the rather grand entrance of Wave Hill opens into a soaring atrium; on either side are long wings containing different growing zones. The extensive collections within include tropical plants, succulents, fuchsias, orchids, and overwintering topiary.

When money is no object, a magnificent 'sun castle' is the result. This two-story extravaganza incorporates many of the traditional greenhouse features—vented windows with arched gothic framing, a vaulted ceiling—with clearly theatrical elements such as turrets, balconies, and flying pennants.

The solar greenhouse in Helen and Scott Nearing's walled garden in Maine was built to provide vegetables year-round. The walls are of local stone and an old-fashioned split door can provide ventilation. In this photo, the growing beds house tomato plants; annuals such as poppies and sunflowers naturally reseed themselves in the greenhouse.

Of more typically modest proportions, this alumimun-frame kit greenhouse still provides plenty of room for storage, propagation benches, and hanging plants. The combination of shade cloth, vents, and fans fulfill the same function of climate control as found in much grander models.

A WORLD APART

Greenhouses are often divided into two categories: those that are attached to the house and those that stand alone in the garden.

If you build the structure separate from your main residence, you must ensure safe access for people, and for utilities such as water, electricity, or gas lines. But practical considerations aside, a freestanding greenhouse can also become a destination in the garden, integral to the design of the landscape, and perhaps even a restful place from which to escape and spend time alone in the greenery.

In a mild or tropical climate a greenhouse or conservatory can be used year-round, not only to protect the most delicate and tender plants from storms but also to provide a venue for outdoor entertaining. This model was constructed atop a wooden deck surround. With the doors flung open and plenty of night lighting, it becomes the perfect place for cocktails.

Why not place the greenhouse truly away from it all? The owners of this one decided to house it near the beach, where they can enjoy views out over the water while tending their plants. As long as you provide comfortable and practical access—here in the form of a wide, level brick pathway—supplies and plants can easily be delivered to and from the garden proper.

Even in Florida, where tropical plants abound, there are many uses for a greenhouse. This structure was used to house shade-loving orchids. Such plants that favor lower light conditions can be kept well-shaded by a permanent lath roof.

Although this greenhouse stands out in the garden, the structure has been thoughtfully integrated into a formal garden design. The boxwood-enclosed square beds and the paving neatly intersected with brick echo the lines of the greenhouse.

This garden may look low-maintenance but there's still plenty to keep the gardener busy in this spacious greenhouse. A special collection of moisture-loving tropicals, for instance, would thrive in a humid indoor environment. Conversely, if your climate is damp and cool but you crave a room full of desert plants, you can adjust temperature and humidity levels inside your greenhouse to provide ideal growing conditions for cacti and succulents.

ATTACHED TO THE HOUSE

A greenhouse or conservatory that is connected to the main house calls for the same basic construction techniques used in freestanding structures but offers several advantages. It becomes essentially a new extension—a garden room—raising the total square footage of the home and tying into the house utilities.

Not all attached greenhouses are fully integrated with the house; many simply incorporate an exterior house wall rather than a fourth glazed side; these are referred to as 'lean-to' greenhouses. Although you may tie into the house electrical and plumbing systems, you can enter it only from the garden. A lean-to can also share a wall with a garage, shed, or fence—any walled structure that can support it. Glass-to-ground construction allows more growing space than knee walls.

ABOVE: A sunny room addition can serve as a practial adjunct to the house. Consider adapting a modest-size lean-to greenhouse as an entryway to the front door, a mud room or ante-room to the kitchen. Container plants such as herbs flourish year-round, tender plants can find a winter home, and the waterproof floor tolerates a little trekked-in dirt.

Increasingly popular are glass-walled rooms that can be accessed from within the main dwelling and which are in essence another room in the house. These most often follow the conservatory model, providing comfortable surroundings for dining or relaxing rather than serving as practical spaces for propagating plants or storing supplies. Conservatories can also house a specialty plant collection, such as orchids, which can easily be admired and tended daily.

Tucked away in the woods, with careful landscaping surrounding it, this angled sunroom provides peaceful views of spring unfolding in the garden. Shaded by deciduous trees in summer, then warmed after leaves drop in winter, the roof must be cleared of leaf debris each fall. Branches are pruned up and away from the structure to guard against damage caused by falling limbs as a result of wind storms or the weight of snow.

Fully custom-designed, this conservatory is truly an extension of the house and contains many enhanced features. The tile floor provides radiant heat, while ceiling fans, electronically controlled vents, and an air conditioning unit keep the air cool during the California summer. The room is as carefully decorated as any other in the house, with beautiful lighting fixtures, furnishings, and plants displayed in gracious containers.

This wooden model is very much a working greenhouse and differs only from a stand-alone model in lacking the fourth glazed wall and roof span. Placed against a south- or west-facing wall, however, the fully glazed roof allows in plenty of light and heat for the seedlings and potted plants inside. There's also room for storage under the benches, and a warm wall against which to put tender plants when frost threatens.

TUCKED AWAY

Where should your greenhouse go? First of all, you must take sun, weather patterns, and building codes into account (page 20). You must also ensure reasonable access for people and supplies.

But that doesn't mean the structure needs to be front and center. There are many ways to incorporate a greenhouse into even the smallest garden. And creative use of plants, both permanent and annual, will soften the outlines of the structure, making it look more at home in the landscape.

If your lot is small, remember that lean-to greenhouses are great space savers. Don't ignore side yards or utility areas, either; make use of an out-of-the-way spot.

A cottage garden needs a greenhouse—the abundance that is characteristic of this style demands plenty of plant material from the gardener. Greenhouses can be used to store and propagate bulbs, start young perennials, and take cuttings from roses and other shrubs. This garden also features plenty of portable plants, such as the potted cyclamen, which can be brought into the greenhouse for an even longer period of bloom.

Another way to make a greenhouse seem at home is to link its style to the main house or another 'hardscape' feature, such as a wall, fence, or deck. This wooden greenhouse sits on the patio and was painted to match the house trim. The result is a tidy and integrated piece of architecture.

This working greenhouse is placed against the edge of the garden, with a fence behind. Plantings on either side reach no higher than halfway up the glazing walls and the perimeter is kept clear of plants to discourage insects from entering. A curved path is wide enough to permit wheelbarrow access, but continues past the greenhouse, making the structure seem to be just one element of the garden, rather than a focal point.

Why not surround your greenhouse with a riot of plants? Trees, clipped shrubs, and perennials virtually obscure this greenhouse, but plants are carefully pruned to prevent any damage to the glazing. Remember that you can always use supplemental lighting to provide warmth and light to your indoor plants (page 40).

INSIDE VIEW

The most common complaint of greenhouse gardeners is that their activities soon outgrow their space, as they rapidly find new plants and new uses for the structure. It pays to build the largest greenhouse you can, and to organize and outfit it according to its intended use.

There are as many ways to design the interior of your greenhouse as there are ways to rearrange your living room furniture —but the two most important items are sturdy, well-placed plant benches and properly planned storage areas. Greenhouse gardening requires special tools, containers, potting mixes, fertilizers, and other supplies. If you have adequate storage, all of these materials will be at your fingertips and ready for use.

Automate as many systems as possible within the greenhouse. In fact, there are alternatives to just about every manual task, from venting to watering, heating, cooling, adding humidity or even fertilizing your plants. But consider what you will be growing. Humidity systems are really only necessary for tropical moisture-loving plants. Cactus and succulents rarely need automatic irrigation. And if you use your greenhouse only for getting a jump start on the spring growing season, you're unlikely to need elaborate heating or cooling devices.

The generous interior space of a gothic arch greenhouse allows for a wide range of growing styles. This lovely place houses every conceivable type of plant: climbing vines, staked vegetables, flowering plants in containers, herbs, shade-loving plants beneath the benches, and even growing bags for tomatoes. The result is a lush combination of edible and ornamental bounty.

One of the primary purposes for the greenhouse is to provide a place for starting plants that you will transplant outdoors or display in your home. You can use the space to start bulbs such as paperwhites, grow divided perennials until they are large enough for transplanting, and start houseplants such as African violets from seed.

This greenhouse shows how much can be achieved by going vertical. Grapes and tomatoes happily reach up towards the roof. You can control the size of such rapid growers by placing them in containers and pinching back the growing shoots. And by rotating a variety of vegetables and flowering plants over time, you can ensure a diverse environment that helps to keep the greenhouse free of unwanted pests and diseases.

A kit greenhouse can be transformed into a little hideaway; a place to peruse gardening catalogs and have a cup of tea or sip lemonade while you tend to your growing plant collection. You can divide the space into different growing zones: on one side could be propagation benches, the other might provide a display area for your favorite flowers.

Whether or not you are comfortable wielding a portable drill or a circular saw, you'll probably want to get involved in the construction of your new greenhouse. At the very least, an understanding of the basic building elements will help you to choose a structure that will suit your taste

BUILDING
BASICS

and budget. But these are not the only factors that should influence your decision.

The climate inside the greenhouse must be carefully controlled in order for plants to grow well. In fact, the amount and type of sunlight that reaches your plants, the greenhouse temperature, and the humidity are determined by the exterior design and the interior details. That's why it's important to clarify what you intend to grow, and when. Then you can decide on such details as glazing type, a foundation, vents and windows, and interior systems such as misters, supplemental lighting, heaters, coolers, and automated irrigation.

Building a greenhouse is much like building any other garden structure: You work from the ground up and the outside in. Start with preparation of the site, then put in the foundation and utilities, if needed, and then proceed to the actual construction of the walls, roof, and glazing.

This well-built greenhouse extends the growing season in Gig Harbor, Washington.

BE YOUR OWN BUILDER

Constructing a greenhouse yourself may sound like a daunting task, but if you are handy with tools and you enjoy building, you can certainly assemble a greenhouse kit in a few weekends. Designing and building a greenhouse from scratch obviously requires more construction experience.

To determine how large a greenhouse you need, visualize the many ways you might use it. Is it a season-extender or do you want year-round climate control? Are you expecting to grow a large collection of specialty plants? Would you like an indoor-outdoor room in which you can relax? Although many greenhouses can be enlarged later, it is generally better and more economical to build the largest greenhouse you can from the beginning. Rare is the gardener who complains of too much empty space in the greenhouse.

The structures illustrated on pages 94–109 will give you a good idea of the range of styles available. Additional sources of hobby greenhouse kits and supplies can be found on page 110.

BEFORE YOU BEGIN

If you are building a simple freestanding greenhouse from a kit, it's unlikely that you'll need any planning permission. But it's wise to consult your local building authority (usually in the city or county administration) before you buy or build a greenhouse to determine whether you need any permits and what, if any, building codes or zoning bylaws apply to your project. You may need to have both your plans and your building project evaluated for the following:

- Electrical and plumbing installations
- Construction safety issues, such as the size and strength of the greenhouse frame
- Footings or foundations
- Setback distance from property lines
- Allowed square footage in relation to your site
- Height in relation to surrounding structures and your neighbor's views
- Fire resistance

KIT GREENHOUSES

Although many companies make fine greenhouse kits, not all of them provide adequate instructions or assistance. Before you buy a greenhouse, ask to see the instruction manual. Are the directions clear? Does it contain good illustrations, photography, or a video that clearly demonstrate how the kit is assembled? Is there a list of materials and any tools you will need? Are you required to purchase any additional materials, or does it arrive with all supplies and hardware? And finally, does the manufacturer or supplier have a help line that you can call for assistance?

When you receive a kit, lay out all the sections so you can check them against the materials list. Separate any unmarked pieces and group similar parts together. Read the manual carefully and seek clarification from the manufacturer or dealer if needed before you begin—it's much too easy to assemble an entire frame and then realize that you incorrectly installed a key component along the way.

ADDING ON

You can also build a greenhouse or even a conservatory upon an existing deck or porch. Be sure that the structure can support the heavy load, that the wood is sound, and that good drainage can be provided. If erecting a greenhouse on a paved patio, also be sure that you'll have sufficient drainage and that the slab is sufficiently thick to bear the structure's weight without cracking.

If you order a kit greenhouse through the mail, don't be alarmed when just a small box or two arrive on your doorstep. Manufacturers typically send the kits disassembled to minimize shipping costs. The first thing you should do is open the box and inspect the contents against the packing list, checking for any damaged or missing components.

USING PROFESSIONALS

You may need professional help if your project is substantial or if you are inexperienced in building techniques. What kind of assistance can you expect?

CUSTOM DESIGN: An architect or a custom greenhouse-design firm is particularly helpful if you are adding on to your existing house or if you want a greenhouse that blends well with your house architecture.

ENGINEER: If your property features elevation changes or has drainage or soil problems, you should contact a structural engineer. It may be necessary to install an underground drainage system, or to plan carefully to prevent erosion or collapse of a slope. Another option is to construct a "pit" greenhouse that can be set into a slope (page 96).

BUILDING CONTRACTOR: Choose a builder who is familiar with greenhouse materials and construction, even if you are building from a kit. Greenhouse manufacturers, engineers, and architects can often give you good references for a local building contractor.

ELECTRICIAN: If you use no other professionals, hire a qualified electrician to ensure that your greenhouse is powered safely, especially if you are connecting to an existing electrical panel or require installation of underground conduit.

PLUMBING: You will use a lot of water in the greenhouse. A reliable plumbing system will be invaluable. A plumber can help you plan and install faucets, automated irrigation, and a misting system, if desired.

In all cases, it's wise to contact former clients of the professionals you are considering, and find out whether they were satisfied with the work; ask if you can come and inspect their greenhouse for yourself. Always insist on a written, signed quote before the job begins, and then sign a contract for the specific work to be done. Don't assume that a professional will always work to code and comply with building inspections; insist that they do so.

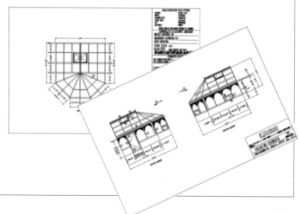

PROPER PLACEMENT

Although your garden may not offer the ideal place for a greenhouse, you should still look for the best possible location on your site. Of primary importance is light— find a spot that receives at least four hours of direct sunlight during the winter months.

PROVIDING UTILITIES

Bringing water and electricity to an attached greenhouse is simple if the household utilities can be extended into the new structure. Underground pipes can deliver water to a freestanding greenhouse, but should be buried below the frost line or as specified by code. Bringing electricity to a freestanding greenhouse from the main house panel is a job best left to an electrician (page 36). Rain barrels that collect and store water are an excellent irrigation source.

NEARBY PLANTINGS

While a nearby deciduous tree can provide welcome dappled shade in the summer, its bare trunk and branches will cast a shadow in the winter and block some light. And remember that if your greenhouse is near any tree, you will have to clear litter from the roof periodically. Even evergreens shed needles, leaves, and other debris. Evergreen hedges and trees, however, do a fine job of reducing winds.

WIND AND WEATHER

Prevailing winds provide cooling and ventilation in the summer. High winds, however, can cause heat loss in winter and compromise the stability of the greenhouse. If you live in a windy area, tie the structure tightly to the foundation and choose a strong glazing material.

Siting the greenhouse in an open area or on a slope will expose it to more of the elements than an area sheltered by buildings or windbreaks. The bottom of a hill or a hollow provides more shelter, but can also be wet or prone to early frosts. Lean-to greenhouses attached to the house are subject to roof runoff and snow slides, which may call for extra gutters and an unbreakable roof glazing such as polycarbonate.

N

EXPOSURE

The sun's rays penetrate the greenhouse most strongly when they are perpendicular to the glazing. To get the maximum amount of light, one long side of the greenhouse should face within a 20° angle of true south. However, the precise orientation of a freestanding greenhouse is not critical because it receives light from all sides. A southeastern or eastern exposure allows in the most morning light. If you live in a very hot summer climate, a north-south orientation may be best.

For a lean-to or conservatory, south facing, southeast-facing, or east-facing walls will provide the greatest light exposure. A western exposure will provide enough light, but the hot afternoon sun may make cooling the structure more difficult in summer. A north-facing greenhouse will provide enough sunlight only for plants with low light requirements.

WITHIN EASY REACH

Chances are you'll be building your greenhouse when there's no snow on the ground, but don't forget that you'll also be trudging out to it on cold winter days. Unless you're prepared to shovel a long path to your baby plants, make sure that the greenhouse is as close as possible to entryways for access, and to driveways for delivering supplies. If you will use your greenhouse primarily to start seedlings and for propagation, place it near your flower and vegetable garden.

STABLE SURFACE

The ground should be firm and easily compacted to provide a level building surface. If the soil is unstable, the greenhouse will be subject to shifting, which could warp or break the glazing and framing. Place your greenhouse away from potentially invasive tree roots, such as those of honey locust, which can disturb the greenhouse foundation.

GROWING GREENHOUSES

My love affair with plants started innocently enough. A co-worker gave me a cutting from an arrowhead *(Syngonium)*. I took it home and stuck it in a glass of water, and it rooted. Mildly surprised, I dug some soil out of my yard, sifted it for rocks, and carefully planted my arrowhead. I was so pleased when it put out new leaves that I started taking cuttings from that one plant, rooting them, and placing the pots throughout my apartment. Soon the plants were competing for space with my books.

After this success with a single plant, I decided to diversify. Weekends were devoted to visiting local nurseries to see what I could bring home. Success with Swedish ivy, wandering Jew, and philodendron stimulated my desire for more exotic plants. Dieffenbachia, purple passion *(Gynura sarmentosa)*, rubber trees and Ficus came next. I didn't meet with success with all the plants—believe me I killed my fair share! But I learned a lot. Ferns need watering twice a week but Swedish ivy doesn't. Ficus loves the sun but the foliage of dieffenbachias burns easily. And all houseplants hate garden soil. Soft and pliable in the garden, my soil turned rock-hard when I put into pots. I wanted to give my plants the very best, so I started mixing my own potting soil of equal parts peat moss, vermiculite, and perlite, but soon switched to a professional potting mixture.

MY FIRST GREENHOUSE

And I kept buying plants. Begonias became a passion. I loved the highly patterned foliage of the rexes and the growth habits of the rhizomatous types, I was enchanted by the flowers of the tuberous and Reigers. I began to collect peperomias and then ferns and then cacti and then and then ... well, y'all can guess how it ended! Because of my plant "addiction," I was forced to sell some of my more common specimens. We still outgrew my apartment. I started looking for a house, and finally found one that had lots of windows and a backyard large enough to put in a greenhouse.

The first winter, I crowded the plants that couldn't fit upstairs into a cold basement area and maintained them through the winter under fluorescent lights. Although I sustained only few losses, I was almost as miserable as my plants, and I vowed not to endure another winter without a greenhouse.

The next spring I started building a simple structure with a frame of treated 2-by-4s. It measured 16 feet by 12 feet and had a fiberglass roof. I stapled plastic film inside and out, and at one end I hung a gas heater from supports. It took most of the summer to build, what with buying more plants (after all, I was going to have a greenhouse), tending the ones I already had, and working full time. Finally the greenhouse was finished—just in time for cold weather.

I learned a lot about greenhouses that winter: how it was critical that heat circulate evenly; that hot air must not blow directly on any plants; that good ventilation reduces humidity levels and thus controls fungal diseases; and that the heater must be large

Libby Rich has been in business for 26 years in Birmingham, Alabama. She is the author of The Odyssey Book of Houseplants *and regularly appears on a local television station to discuss her favorite plants. Her passion remains unabated.*

enough to warm the greenhouse when temperatures drop to unexpected lows. I learned that when planning a greenhouse you must either control your urge to buy everything or build the structure twice as large. I stumbled through that first experience and emerged more determined than ever to get it right.

SECOND TIME AROUND

Fate intervened 25 years ago when I was laid off from my job. I decided to try and make a living doing something I loved, so I opened a plant shop in a tiny storefront on a busy street in Birmingham. This of course called for a new greenhouse. My second version was a 50-by-100-foot lean-to. This time I had two heaters suspended from the ceiling, strategically placed circulating fans, benches designed to hold a maximum number of plants, and thermostatically controlled vents.

Fortunately the store did well, and I found that not only could I increase my personal plant collection, but I could build a larger greenhouse. Better yet, I could pay someone else to build it. This 300-by-100-foot version was constructed by a professional builder. It had a double glazing of plastic film continuously filled with air, an evaporative cooler, and a thermostat alarm.

FOURTH TIME'S THE CHARM

With more than 3,000 square feet in which to grow plants, I was in hog heaven! In the mean time my tiny storefront quadrupled in size, and I began to sell annuals, herbs, and perennials. It took ten years for me to outgrow those greenhouses, but sure enough, once again I found myself out of room.

I purchased 28,500 square feet of land two blocks from the original store and promptly covered a quarter of it with greenhouses. These are permanent structures with sturdy steel framing and fiberglass roof glazing. Water faucets are located every 20 feet, fertilizer injectors stand by for weekly use, insect problems are dispatched promptly with an industrial sprayer, heaters are connected to thermostat alarms, ventilating fans control humidity, and circulating fans distribute the heat evenly. A back-up generator ensures that fans and heaters will run even if the power goes out.

The demands of running a business have cut into the private time I have with my plants. But still, some mornings I get up early just so that I can be alone in the greenhouse. I open the door and the sweet fragrance of the earth greets me. Surrounded by beautiful greenery, I wander around. I stroke the delicate foliage of a maidenhair fern, untwine creeping figs from their neighbors, remove a dead flower from a gardenia. I am content, for finally I have enough room for the addiction that I will never outgrow.

Syngonium podophyllum

A SOLID FOUNDATION

The purpose of a foundation is to anchor the greenhouse securely to the ground. Temporary or portable greenhouses often rely on anchor stakes to hold down the structure. Most greenhouses, however, need more permanent support. If you buy a kit, ask the greenhouse manufacturer which type of foundation is best suited for your area. And always check the local building codes to find out how deep your foundation must go.

LAYING OUT THE SITE

No matter what kind of foundation or base you are building, the site must be level and the foundation must be square. Generally, the greenhouse floor level should be slightly higher than grade, to aid drainage. If you are planning to pour a concrete slab or build a low-level deck, you must first excavate all topsoil from the site. If not, remember to plan your in-ground bed locations in advance and amend the soil as necessary.

To get a rough layout of the foundation, first drive stakes into the four corners of the site. Construct batterboards from 1-by-2-inch lumber and

place them behind the stakes, outside the foundation area. Then stretch string between the batterboards.

Make sure the dimensions of the intersecting strings are correct for the foundation, and that the diagonal measurements from corner to corner are equal, or measure the corner angles as shown below.

When your measurements are final, transfer them to the ground with a plumb bob, and remove the corner stakes. Remove the string to excavate the foundation, then replace it to guide you in constructing the foundation.

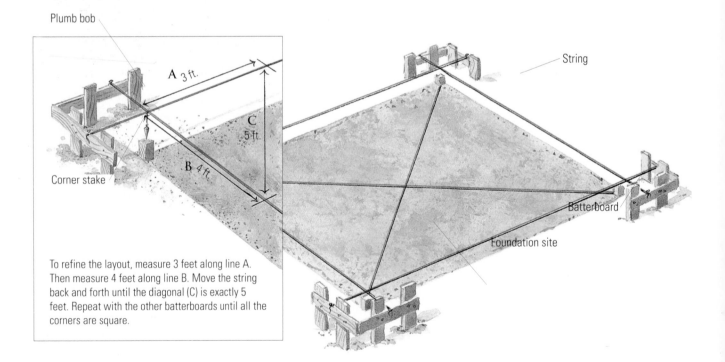

Plumb bob

A 3 ft.

C 5 ft.

B 4 ft.

Corner stake

String

Batterboard

Foundation site

To refine the layout, measure 3 feet along line A. Then measure 4 feet along line B. Move the string back and forth until the diagonal (C) is exactly 5 feet. Repeat with the other batterboards until all the corners are square.

WOOD FOUNDATIONS

For greenhouses under 240 square feet, you can simply bolt together pressure-treated lumber as a base. You then bolt the frame of the greenhouse to the base. For a 6-by-8-foot greenhouse, one tier of timbers is sufficient; for a 10-by-12-foot structure, two tiers are best. For added strength, insert 2-foot lengths of rebar into the ground inside the wooden base, and fasten them to the lumber with metal (EMT) straps or conduit "J" nails.

Another option is to build a low-level wooden deck and place the greenhouse upon it. This deck increases ventilation through the greenhouse, but it also increases the likelihood that insects, snails, and other pests will enter the structure; you can cover the deck surface with plywood to prevent this. The wooden deck posts can be sunk into concrete or anchored to concrete piers, but in a frost-free climate another option is metal post spikes—essentially post anchors on pointed stakes.

STRONGER FOUNDATIONS

A more substantial foundation is called for if the greenhouse is larger than 12 by 20 feet or is glazed with glass. The options then are to pour a concrete slab, pour a continuous concrete footing around the perimeter, or build a footing of concrete block.

As an alternative to a continuous concrete footing, you also can sink precast piers into concrete footings set every few feet around the perimeter, or install post anchors into footings that you have cast in fiber-form tubes.

A concrete slab can be reinforced with wire mesh and should be at least 3 inches thick, with thicker perimeter footings. All footings should extend down below the frost line to prevent damage that can twist the greenhouse frame and crack the glazing.

For added weatherproofing, coat the foundation with waterproofing compound or underlay a concrete slab with a polyethylene moisture barrier. To retain heat and protect the foundation, surround it with belowground rigid insulation panels. Suitable insulation includes 1- or 2-inch polystyrene or polyurethane board.

In any case, you will need to excavate for a footing that is twice the width of the walls or sills on which the greenhouse will sit. If you are pouring concrete, the trench must also be big enough to accommodate the necessary wooden forms. Remember that you must install your utility lines before you pour a concrete foundation, so excavate deeply enough to bury plumbing and electrical conduit.

A concrete block footing should extend at least 6 inches above grade, but you can build it up higher as a knee wall.

The greenhouse must be tied to the foundation or footings, usually by means of anchor bolts that you embed in the wet concrete. Another alternative is to embed a wooden board in the wet

You can construct a knee wall of poured concrete, concrete block, brick, or mortared stone, as shown here. Whatever the material, the wall must be anchored securely to the footing beneath it. In cold-winter areas, you can cover the interior of the knee wall with insulation panels to retain heat.

concrete. When the foundation has cured, the board will be stable enough for you to bolt the framing to it.

KNEE WALLS

If you opt for a knee wall (also called a pony wall or a base wall) rather than a glass-to-ground model, keep in mind that you'll lose the growing space underneath the benches (except possibly for growing mushrooms). A knee wall has other advantages, however. It protects the bottom glazing and adds height to the interior of the greenhouse, including a kit greenhouse. Attached greenhouses often use a knee wall to match an existing foundation or to raise the greenhouse to the floor level of a building. And a knee wall provides a convenient location for installing electrical wiring and outlets.

FLOORING

A greenhouse floor must drain well, and it must provide good footing as it is likely to be wet much of the time. An earthen floor will be constantly muddy and weedy, so your walkways should have some other material covering them. Place a layer of pea gravel underneath the walkway and the benches. If you make the gravel layer deep enough, it can also function as a heat sink, giving back at night some of the heat collected during the day.

Several flooring options are shown here. A paved surface makes it easiest to move carts or wheelbarrows but can be slipperier when wet. The same is true of wooden decking, but you can install strips of nonslip material directly onto the wood.

With planning, it is even possible to have a heated floor in a greenhouse. The procedure is similar to that used for floor-heated garages. Either electrical cables are buried, or hot water is fed into PVC pipes buried beneath the greenhouse floor. You should discuss this option with a builder.

Masonry materials such as pavers, flagstone, and cobblestone are often found in older greenhouses. You can create this antique look yourself even in a newer structure by mixing and matching tile, used brick, and stone, as was done here. Underlay the material with a firm base of sand.

Another feature of old-fashioned greenhouses and conservatories is the cast-iron heating grill shown here. Contemporary versions of this flooring are available through custom design firms, especially those that specialize in conservatories.

One of the most practical choices for a modern greenhouse is to install some kind of concrete patio pavers or blocks. These are available in a range of sizes and shapes, including the large squares shown here, and can be laid in a bed of sand.

FLOOR DRAIN

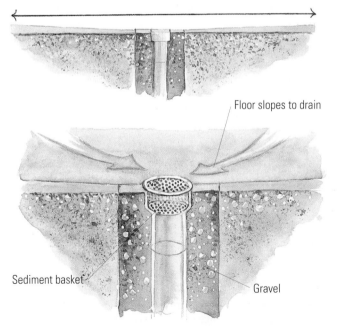

Floor slopes to drain

Sediment basket

Gravel

Wooden floors are much like exposed decking and should be made of naturally decay-resistant or pressure-treated lumber. Lay the 2-by-4-inch or 2-by-6-inch boards on crosspieces set 2 feet apart. Leave a slight gap between boards for drainage.

If the greenhouse is placed on a concrete slab, the floor must slope to a drain. A floor drain may lead to an underground pipe that channels water to a sewer line or directly outdoors, or you can create a drain several feet deep in a gravel pit, as shown above. In either case, install a sediment basket to prevent the drain from becoming clogged.

FRAMING OPTIONS

Aluminum is the most popular choice for greenhouse framing and is used in many mid-price-range kit greenhouses. Wood, however, is the most common material used for building a greenhouse from a plan.

METAL

Aluminum greenhouse framing is extruded into shapes to accommodate various glazing systems and connectors. The extrusions provide channels for condensation runoff, for attaching accessories, and for the expansion and contraction of some plastic glazing. Aluminum is lightweight, strong, and corrosion-resistant, and it requires little maintenance. Some manufacturers offer a more attractive choice of anodized or color-enameled aluminum framing.

Galvanized steel beams or tubing may also serve as greenhouse framing. They provide a strong, rigid frame that is somewhat heavier than aluminum and can support a greater roof load. The rollformed beams allow for condensation runoff. Because steel frames rust, some are galvanized to protect against corrosion.

The main drawback of metal frames is their high thermal conductivity, which allows heat to transfer out of the greenhouse through the framework, thereby increasing interior condensation and raising heating costs. "Thermal breaks" built into the glazing bars can help solve this problem; they separate the outside and inside metal to prevent direct contact.

Generally, you bolt the bottom members of a metal frame to a wooden or metal sill. Dissimilar metals should not be used in close contact when constructing a metal greenhouse frame because electrolysis can cause corrosion.

WOOD

Wood is readily available, attractive, and familiar to most people who are handy with tools. It provides a better thermal barrier to heat loss than metal. The drawback of wooden framing is that it requires regular maintenance.

Redwood, Western red cedar, and cypress are naturally rot-resistant woods commonly used to frame greenhouses. You can also use lumber that has been pressure-treated with either CCA (chromate copper arsenate) or ACQ (ammoniac copper quat), but don't use wood that has been treated with creosote or pentachlorophenol. Treated lumber can be painted to seal the wood—white paint reflects the most light around the greenhouse.

Most wood-framed greenhouses call for platform construction techniques. First you assemble the walls on a flat surface, then fasten them to the sill. Finally, you add the roof. A faster and cheaper method for larger greenhouses is post-and-beam construction. With this method, you connect the main structural posts—usually 4-by-4-inch or 4-by-6-inch pressure-treated lumber—to the foundation or to concrete footings. The posts support the roof girders and rafters or trusses. You then fasten wooden timbers between the posts to support the siding. Precise measurements are less critical with this building style because adjustments can be made as the work progresses.

You can nail and bolt together your wood-framed greenhouse, or you can use the same metal connecting plates as commonly employed in deck construction.

PLASTIC

Rigid PVC (polyvinyl chloride) framing works well for small, lightweight greenhouses. It's generally not considered the most aesthetic option, but it is the most economical. PVC doesn't rust or corrode, but it's also not as strong as other types of framing. Over time the plastic becomes weak, and it may also be difficult to maintain a connection to a wooden sill or foundation. Only film and flexible plastic can be used to glaze a PVC frame.

The familiar PVC plumbing pipe can be used to frame a home-built greenhouse, and smaller-diameter flexible PVC pipe can be used for "hoop house" construction (page 94). Joining sections of PVC pipe is relatively easy, but the shape of the greenhouse will be limited by the configuration of available pipe connectors.

DOORS AND WINDOWS

Properly speaking, the "windows" in a greenhouse are also the walls, but it's not unusual to find several different kinds of windows, vents, and glazing in a single structure.

You can purchase both awning (top-hinged) and louvered window vents from greenhouse suppliers. Normally, you put awning windows on the roof, but they can also be placed in the sides of the greenhouse. Another option is to install louvered vents for added ventilation. On a small greenhouse, awning and louvered window vents may be operated either manually or with an automatic vent opener (page 32).

Most home-built greenhouses and many kit greenhouses have hinged doors. The advantages are simpler construction and a tighter seal between interior and exterior. The drawback is that whether a door opens outward or inward, a gust of wind can cause it to slam, possibly damaging the door or even the greenhouse itself. If you live in an area with prevailing winds, try to face your greenhouse door away from them. Aluminum kit greenhouses frequently have either single or double sliding doors. These doors are unaffected by wind and allow easy access, although debris in the track or worn bearings can cause them to stick.

Greenhouse doors may be fully glazed, half-glazed, or solid. Some greenhouses have combination screen doors that help provide ventilation while keeping out insects. All doors should be weather-stripped to minimize drafts.

This greenhouse was built almost entirely of recycled materials. The 50-year-old redwood windows were salvaged from an old military base; the door came from a house demolition. The owner employed post-and-beam construction, fitting the windows into a grid formed by the beams and horizontal rails. The rear wall partially incorporates an adjacent chimney for added warmth.

GLAZING CHOICES

You may choose one type of glazing for the walls and another for the roof. Base your selection on the different properties of the material, such as strength or the ability to navigate curved eaves.

GLASS

Many gardeners still favor the traditional greenhouse glazing. It is stable, nonflammable, easy to work with, and lets in almost all available light. However, glass is also breakable, conducts heat and cold easily, and has a higher initial cost. The heavy weight of a glass greenhouse requires a strong frame and foundation.

Your choice of glass will depend upon your climate and how the glass will be used. Glass is available in single, double, and triple strengths. It's best to use tempered glass, which is much stronger than ordinary glass, in and around doors and for the roof of an all-glass greenhouse—if it breaks, it forms small sections of glass rather than shattering into sharp pieces. There are several types of insulated double and triple glass, usually with spacers between each layer or laminated with a layer of plastic.

PLASTICS

POLYCARBONATE AND ACRYLIC PANELS are lightweight and have the highest light transmission of all plastic glazing. Both are available in single and double (or "twin") wall panels. Double panels provide greater insulation and admit about 80 percent of available light. Polycarbonate is also available in triple wall panels. Neither plastic yellows significantly over its lifetime (20 years for acrylic and 10 to 15 years for polycarbonate). Both glazing types scratch easily and have high rates of expansion and contraction. Acrylic glazing is the more flexible but also the more flammable of the two. Some panels may be coated or impregnated with a UV-blocking material to resist sun degradation, or with a wetting agent to reduce condensation build up.

FIBERGLASS may be clear or translucent (the familiar green panels). It is available in flat rolls and corrugated panels. Fiberglass is flexible, strong, inexpensive, and easy to work with. With regular applications of a resin coating, it can last up to 20 years, but over time it will yellow and degrade due to pollution and sunlight.

PVC (POLYVINYL CHLORIDE) film is available in rolls from 4 to 6 feet wide. You can also buy translucent PVC corrugated panels. The film has an estimated life of two to five years and should also have UV protection. The panels are strong but have a high expansion rate. Their estimated life is ten years, but they yellow with age.

POLYETHYLENE FILM is the least expensive plastic covering. Many greenhouses glazed with plastic film use a double-wall system for greater heat insulation. The space between the two layers is inflated with outside air blown in by a small, continuously operating fan. Buy film that is 4-6 mil thick and ask for UV-protected film, which lasts from one to three years.

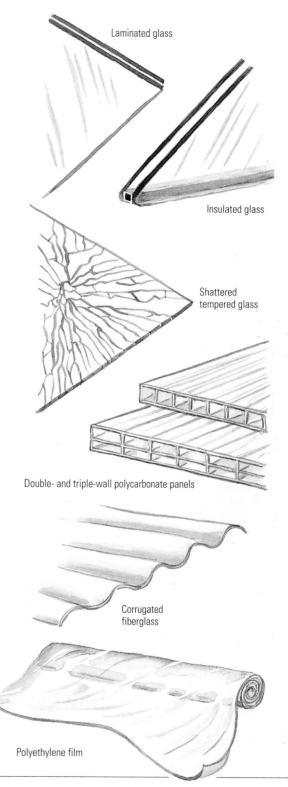

Laminated glass

Insulated glass

Shattered tempered glass

Double- and triple-wall polycarbonate panels

Corrugated fiberglass

Polyethylene film

YOU NEED TO VENT

A supply of fresh air is essential for a healthy greenhouse environment, helping to maintain the temperature, humidity, and carbon dioxide levels that favor plant growth. In addition, well-ventilated plants are less likely to suffer insect and disease infestations. The need for venting is not confined to summer—on a sunny winter day, temperatures in the greenhouse can soar.

Warm air rises naturally by convection in a greenhouse and escapes through individual or continuous roof (or "ridge") vents with the aid of prevailing winds. In a freestanding greenhouse, position roof vents on both sides of the roof. The most effective vents will be those on the side away from the prevailing summer winds.

Louvered or hinged intake vents are generally placed low on greenhouse walls, allowing cooler air to enter and complete the convection cycle. For maximum efficiency the operation of both intake vents and roof vents should be coordinated. Vents can be opened and closed manually or automatically. One kind of automatic device activates the vent with a thermostatically controlled electric motor; another kind consists of a non-electric solar opener that relies on heat buildup to control the vent (heat causes mineral wax in the cylinder to expand, forcing a lever to open the vent).

Roof vents should be about 15 percent larger than intake vents. The total ventilating area (high and low) of an attached greenhouse should equal 25 to 30 percent of the glazed area. In a freestanding greenhouse the roof vents should equal 20 percent of the floor area and intake vents 10 percent. All vents should close tightly. You might want to install window screening to keep out pests (page 88), but screening that is too fine may interfere with airflow.

Venting from the house into an attached greenhouse through interior windows or doors can provide fresh air and help regulate warmth to both buildings.

FANS

You have an alternative to roof vents: an exhaust fan system. The best place for an exhaust fan is high on the end of the greenhouse, away from prevailing winds. The fan operates, in conjunction with low intake vents at the opposite end of the greenhouse to pull fresh air through the greenhouse. The fan evacuates the stale air.

While you can manually activate exhaust fans and intake vents, it's much easier to have them thermostatically controlled. The rate of air exchange required in winter is less than half that of summer in most areas, so a two-speed or variable-speed exhaust fan can be adjusted depending on the season. For maximum effect, do not open roof vents when the exhaust fan is operating.

Circulation fans run all the time to maintain constant horizontal airflow among the plants. Place small "squirrel cage" fans at a height of 8 feet every 10 or 15 feet along the wall so that they all blow in the same direction—they will create a horizontal air flow through the greenhouse. You can also place small fans at ceiling level to blow warm air downward.

Louvers may be made of glass, aluminum, or PVC. Included in most vent systems is a thermostat control, which ensures that louvers open when the temperature reaches a certain point.

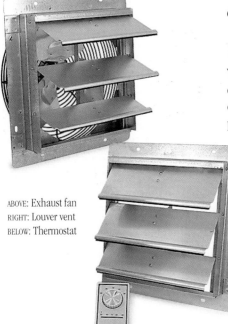

ABOVE: Exhaust fan
RIGHT: Louver vent
BELOW: Thermostat

AIR FLOW

To determine the size of exhaust fan you need, compute the volume of air in your greenhouse. First multiply the structure's width, length, and average height (in feet). The resulting number is the greenhouse volume in cubic feet. Fans are rated by the number of cubic feet of air per minute (cfm.) that they can move. The air in the greenhouse should be changed every 1½ to 2 minutes. For example, if your greenhouse is 10 by 12 by 8 feet, or 960 cubic feet, you will need a fan rated approximately 500 to 700 cfm.

EXHAUST-FAN VENTING

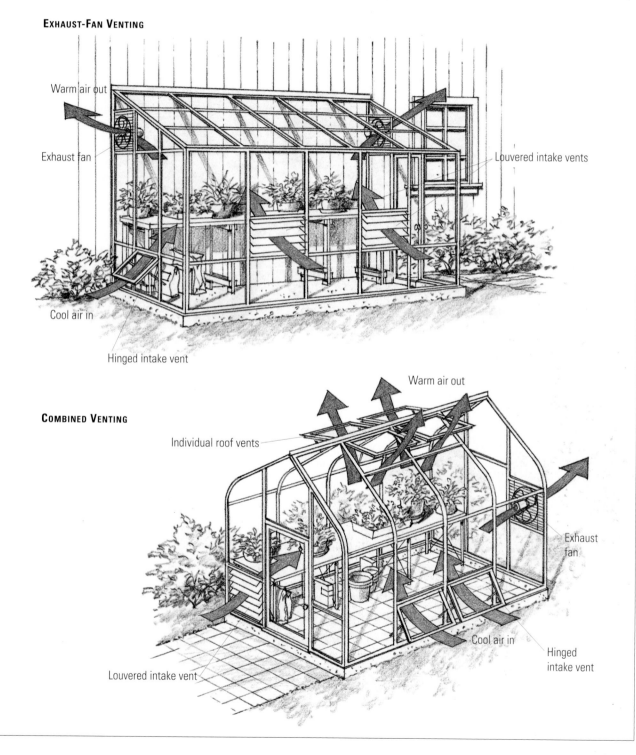

Warm air out

Exhaust fan

Louvered intake vents

Cool air in

Hinged intake vent

COMBINED VENTING

Warm air out

Individual roof vents

Exhaust fan

Cool air in

Hinged intake vent

Louvered intake vent

The shade cloth in this greenhouse is hung in panels in the interior. The fabric panels can be rolled up to adjust the level of shading necessary. The advantage of interior shades is that they don't interfere with roof vents.

During the hottest months of summer, shade paint should be applied liberally and intake louvers opened.

SHADING

Most greenhouses require shading during the summer months to control overheating and to protect the plants from sunburn. There are two methods of shading: by installing shade cloth or by covering the glass with some form of whitewash.

Shade cloth is a material of woven polypropylene, fiberglass, aluminum net, or Mylar that comes in a range of densities from about 40 to 80 percent. Your choice of density will depend upon the light requirements of your plants. The cloth is available in black, white, green, and a green-and-white leaf pattern. Often, kit manufacturers sell shade-cloth systems designed to fit their greenhouses. Exterior roll-up shades of wood, bamboo, or aluminum are another, more expensive, option.

Ideally, shade cloth should be supported by a framework with the top of it a few inches above the roof glazing, but you can also simply drape it over the greenhouse and secure it. You can buy a type of cloth that has grommets around the edges to aid in tying it down; or use clips as fasteners. If you decide to put the shade cloth inside the greenhouse, tack it to wooden framing or clip it to metal roof extrusions.

Whitewash or shading compounds can also be used to provide shade; apply them to the exterior of a glass greenhouse. Latex house paint, diluted with water to any density you like, works well as whitewash, but you may need to reapply it after heavy rains. Remove any remnants of whitewash in the fall by scrubbing it with water and a soft-bristle brush.

CLIMATE CONTROLLERS

Environmental conditions in a greenhouse fluctuate often, and you can find yourself constantly adjusting fans, vents, and watering systems. Fortunately, much of the greenhouse can be operated automatically. Fans and vents can be thermostatically controlled, with vents either motorized or opened by heat-activated pistons. Irrigation, misting, and fogging systems can be activated by timers and humidistats. Controls for these functions can be installed in the greenhouse or integrated into a computerized climate controller that can be manipulated on site or from a remote computer.

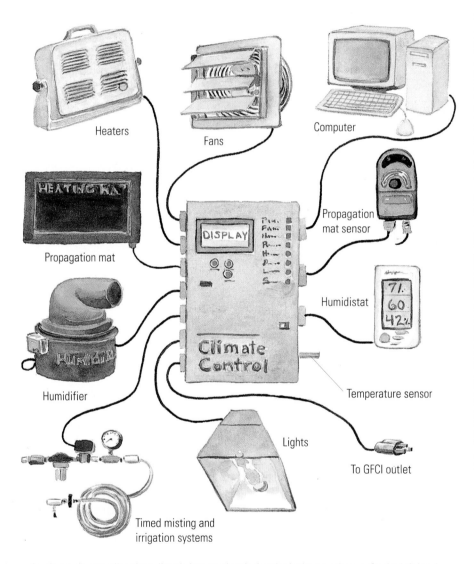

Heaters

Fans

Computer

Propagation mat sensor

Propagation mat

DISPLAY

Humidistat

Humidifier

Climate Control

Temperature sensor

Lights

To GFCI outlet

Timed misting and irrigation systems

An electronic controller plugs directly into an electrical outlet in the greenhouse. On the left-hand side are 120-volt outlets for fans, heaters, propagation mats, humidifiers, misting systems, and lights. On the right-hand side are connections for external sensors, such as a humidistat or propagation-mat sensor. A built-in temperature sensor monitors the temperature, and a programmable timer can activate misters and lights on schedule. The entire unit can be connected to your home computer so that you can monitor the greenhouse or change settings remotely.

SWAMP COOLERS

In warm climates, evaporative coolers (also known as "swamp coolers") are very effective for lowering the temperature in a greenhouse. They are most efficient when the outdoor relative humidity is low. The units are normally wall-mounted on the windward side of the greenhouse, but smaller free-standing models such as the one pictured here can be used in small greenhouses. Cooling occurs when the built-in fan sucks in air and blows it through a wet fibrous pad. As the water in the pad evaporates, the greenhouse temperature can drop as much as 20°F. A reservoir supplies the cooler with water.

POWERING THE GREENHOUSE

Unless you are an electrical engineer or have had considerable wiring experience, you should have your greenhouse electrical system installed by a licensed professional. Before doing any wiring yourself, check local and state electrical codes and local building codes. You may also wish to consult your power company and fire insurance agent.

Normally, you can bring electrical power out to the greenhouse or conservatory from a house service panel and protect it with circuit breakers or fuses. An attached greenhouse requires only a simple extension of the house wiring. For a freestanding greenhouse, an underground waterproof cable must carry the wires. Any wiring circuits brought out to the greenhouse must be properly grounded.

The types of electrical devices in the greenhouse will determine whether you need to install 120-volt or 240-volt service. Fans, humidifiers, fluorescent lights, heating mats and similar devices usually do not draw much current. Small electric heaters and units such as HID (high-intensity discharge) lamps use more current, but a 120-volt circuit is still adequate. You may, however, need additional circuits to service multiple high-draw devices. Check the labels on all equipment for the total number of watts required; be sure that the total wattage does not exceed the capacity of any circuit. Provide enough circuits so that all electrical devices can operate together if needed. A large electric heater or cooler may require a dedicated 240-volt line.

There should be a minimum of one duplex electrical outlet every 8 feet. Some appliances, such as large gable fans and heaters, will require special outlets or may be hard-wired directly to thermostats and panel boxes.

A greenhouse is a wet environment. All greenhouse circuits must be connected to a GFCI (ground fault circuit interrupter) for your protection. In case of an electrical malfunction, or exposure of a unit to water, the GFCI circuit will shut off the current immediately.

UNPOWERED GREENHOUSES

During the winter and even on summer nights, you must find a way to keep the greenhouse warm enough to sustain the plants growing inside. Greenhouses are warmed by the sun's infrared rays, which pass through the glazing to plants, benches, and other objects. There they are converted from light to heat. Warmth is stored within the greenhouse in heat-absorbing materials such as water, masonry, and stone. These heat sinks will slowly return heat to the greenhouse interior as the air temperature drops.

The greenhouse loses heat by conduction through metal framing, by radiation through the glazing at night, and by the infiltration of cold air that replaces the departing warm air. Greenhouses also lose heat through the floor and the foundation, but most heat is lost through the roof. Most double plastic glazing retains heat better than glass. Because heat energy always travels from a warm place to a cold place, there is more heat loss at night or on a cloudy day. A great deal of heat can be lost through vents that have been left open, or through leaks in the glazing panels. Regularly inspect the places where glazing is attached to the framing, and fill gaps with a sealant such as silicone.

Insulated walls and double glazing retain heat better (a second layer of plastic or glass reduces heat loss by about 35 percent), but there may also be a slight loss of available light. A simple and effective seasonal insulating material for a small greenhouse is greenhouse-grade bubble plastic (similar to bubble packing material), which you can attach to the inside of the glazing with a translucent spray adhesive or double-sided tape. You can also line the greenhouse with polyethylene film.

If you have a lean-to greenhouse, you can include a vapor barrier in a solid unglazed wall to prevent cold air from entering the greenhouse and to keep the greenhouse's humid air from entering the walls and eventually causing them to rot. The north wall of a greenhouse, which doesn't provide much light in winter, and the foundation walls can be lined with reflective material or panels that both insulate the walls and reflect the radiant heat.

As a last resort, you can use thermal blankets: Throw them over the greenhouse exterior on unusually cold nights, or install a system of interior pulleys or support bars from which to hang them.

AN ELECTRICAL PLAN

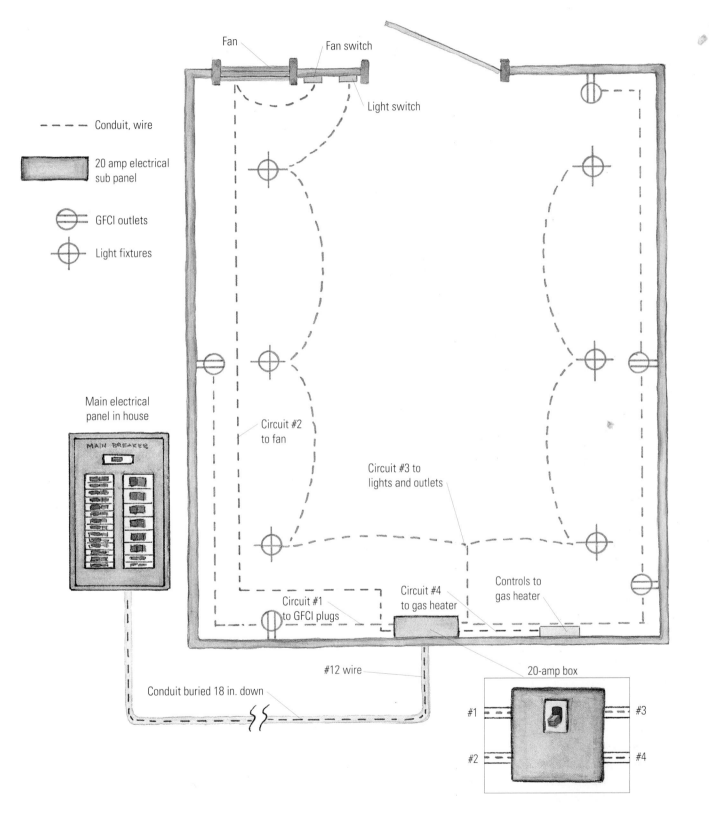

Fan

Fan switch

Light switch

Conduit, wire

20 amp electrical sub panel

GFCI outlets

Light fixtures

Main electrical panel in house

MAIN BREAKER

Circuit #2 to fan

Circuit #3 to lights and outlets

Circuit #1 to GFCI plugs

Circuit #4 to gas heater

Controls to gas heater

#12 wire

Conduit buried 18 in. down

20-amp box

#1   #3

#2   #4

With the vents shut tight, a polycarbonate greenhouse can still maintain an interior temperature that is 10°F warmer than the exterior temperature. However, the addition of even a small portable heater can raise the temperature by 20 or 30°F—usually enough to protect plants from frost damage.

BTU TO YOU TOO

Heat is measured in British thermal units (Btu). The heater's Btu output per hour must be sufficient to replace the heat lost in the greenhouse. Use the following formula to calculate heating requirements for your greenhouse: (A) is the total surface area of the greenhouse in feet (walls and roof). (T) is the difference between the lowest outdoor temperature and the lowest temperature you desire in the greenhouse. (U) is the U-value of your glazing. (The supplier will be able to give you the exact figure, but most glass and polycarbonate has a U-value of about 1.1.) A x T x U = Btus/hour. If your greenhouse is well-insulated, subtract 30 percent from that total. And if the greenhouse is a lean-to and shares a heated wall, subtract another 30 percent. Purchase a heater with a Btu output approximately equal to the total figure.

MAINTAINING WARMTH

The minimum temperature at which you keep your greenhouse will depend on the plants you grow: The greenhouse environment should mimic the natural environment of these plants as closely as possible. In a cool greenhouse this usually translates to 40 to 45°F, in an intermediate-temperature greenhouse it means 55 to 60°F, and a warm greenhouse should be kept at a minimum of 65 to 70°F.

Unless you live in an area with very warm winters or plan to use your greenhouse just for starting seeds in the spring or to overwinter perennials, you will probably want to provide auxiliary heat. Your choice of fuel—whether gas, oil, or electricity—will depend upon its availability and cost where you live. Gas, oil, and wood-burning heaters should be vented to the outside, and fresh air should provide the oxygen needed for combustion. All heaters, including electric ones, should have safety shut-off devices in case of malfunction.

Heaters are usually placed at one end of the greenhouse, and most include a fan blower to circulate the heat. Make sure the blower is capable of pushing warm air to the far end of the greenhouse.

Place thermostats and thermometers half way up a greenhouse wall, and protect them from the sun for accurate performance. A minimum/maximum thermometer registers both high and low temperatures to track the extremes in your greenhouse.

ALARMING INFORMATION

A temperature alarm can save your plants. Some alarm systems are battery-operated; others operate on home current and should have a battery backup. Some can even automatically telephone a service bureau to alert it of a problem. In addition, most home-security systems can incorporate a greenhouse temperature alarm. Put the alarm sensor in a shady, dry place in the greenhouse and the ringer or buzzer where you are most likely to hear it—perhaps inside the house. You select the temperature at which you want the alarm to sound.

OTHER HEAT SOURCES

- *Heating cables* can be used to supply bottom heat to propagation mats and benches. It's considerably cheaper to heat a propagation mat to 70°F than to heat an entire greenhouse.

- *Radiant heat* can be installed in the floor of a greenhouse during construction.

- *Piped hot water* was the traditional means of heating conservatories but is rarely used now.

- *House heat* may be available to a lean-to greenhouse or attached conservatory through an extension of the home's heating system.

- *The sun* can provide up to 25 percent of the heat required by an ordinary greenhouse. Although some specially engineered greenhouses are totally dependent upon the sun for heat, all greenhouses are solar collectors to some extent.

HEATERS

ELECTRIC HEATERS are clean and efficient. They are readily available and easily installed, and can be plugged into either a 120-volt or 240-volt circuit, depending upon the model. Most incorporate a fan and a thermostatic control that can be set to any temperature. The drawbacks of these heaters are the cost of electricity in your locale, and problems associated with power outages.

GAS (NATURAL AND PROPANE) HEATERS may be freestanding, or installed in the greenhouse wall, or hung overhead. While the carbon dioxide they produce might be beneficial to plants, gas heaters must be vented to the outside because they emit fumes such as ethylene and carbon monoxide. Most gas heaters require no electricity and continue to function in a power outage. Some have an electric blower option.

WOOD-BURNING STOVES are still used in some greenhouses. They demand frequent attention and must be vented to the outside.

KEROSENE STOVES require adequate fresh air for complete combustion. They are sometimes used for an emergency backup. Some local for state codes prohibit their use in a greenhouse attached to a dwelling.

TOP: Wall-mounted electric heater.
BOTTOM: Portable electric heater.
LEFT: Gas heater.

For fluorescent light to be effective, it must be set very close to the plants. The minimum distance for most flowering plants is 12 inches from the light source. Smaller plants such as these young orchids benefit from an even closer distance.

WHAT'S A FOOT CANDLE?

The *measurement* of light is based on a somewhat archaic designation known as "foot-candles" (ft-c) or "photometric units" (originally the amount of light from a candle held one foot above a flat object). The *intensity* of the light is measured in lumens per watt. Plants are rated as low, medium, or high in their light requirements.

The amount of light each plant needs depends on its native environment. Plants from the forest floor require low light, for example, while those from open cliffs or fields prosper in bright light. Tall flowering plants may need up to 3,000 ft-c, some foliage plants need as little as 150 ft-c. Medium light is about 1500 ft-c. To be precise, you can purchase a photometer that allows you to measure the number of foot-candles striking a plant's foliage, so you can place your plants where they will receive exactly the amount of light they need.

LET THERE BE LIGHT

Light is essential for photosynthesis—the process by which plants manufacture their food. During the summer months, the average greenhouse receives adequate light for all plant growth. However, during the short days of winter little growth takes place. You can allow your plants to rest during this period, or you can supplement the hours of sunlight with artificial light controlled by a timer.

Tropical plants seem to benefit the most from added light because day and night lengths are almost equal near the equator. However, keep in mind that the length of the night is the trigger for a few plants, such as poinsettia and kalanchoe, to bloom. Their light cycle must not be interrupted for even a few hours. Plans with a sensitive light cycle are referred to as "long-night" (short-day) or "short-night" (long-day) plants. "Day-neutral" plants, such as African violets, cucumbers, and geraniums, are not affected by the length of the night.

You may also wish to install supplemental light in a greenhouse or conservatory located on the north side of a building, or one that is shaded by large trees or other buildings that prevent it from receiving full sunlight. To further increase the light level in a greenhouse, use bright white, mildew-resistant paint on all unglazed surfaces and furnishings.

LIGHTEN UP

Plants that receive no natural light will need 16 to 18 hours of artificial light each day; if there is some natural light, 12 to 14 hours of supplemental light may be sufficient. Ordinary electric (incandescent) bulbs give off light primarily in the red end of the spectrum and are not particularly useful as supplemental lighting for plants. Marginally more useful are so-called grow lights, special incandescent lights that emit both red and blue wavelengths.

The most common form of supplemental interior light is from fluorescent tubes. Cool-white tubes produce light that is primarily in blue wavelengths that produce good growth. For flowering, add a warm-white tube to supply the red wavelengths. Full-spectrum fluorescent tubes are available at greater cost and emit light that is closer to sunlight. The greatest drawback of fluorescent lights is that they must be within inches of the plants to be effective. They also lose their intensity after a year or two and must be replaced. The advantage of fluorescent bulbs is that they can be installed easily in fixtures available at home supply stores. (Note that some inexpensive shop lights have a small "economy" ballast that is not intended to operate more than a few hours per day.)

Higher artificial light levels come from high-intensity discharge (HID) lamps. These send an electrical current through a vaporized gas of sodium (HPS) or metal halide (MH) that is under high pressure. HPS lamps are the brightest and most efficient, but they give off a yellow light that some gardeners find unpleasant. The white light from MH lamps is the artificial light closest to sunlight; in fact, you can get a sunburn if you work under them unprotected. These lights also give off a lot of heat, and they should have a protective glass covering because they can explode if there is an electrical short circuit. Keep in mind that HID lamps are very large and consume substantial amounts of electricity.

Window greenhouses bring more light into the house, enhancing both the atmosphere and the apparent size of a small space such as a bathroom or kitchen. Although it usually provides sufficient natural light for plants, a window greenhouse can be subject to sudden shifts in temperature due to its compact nature.

Ask the manufacturer how large an area the light from its HID lamp will cover. This small model covers 16 square feet of growing space.

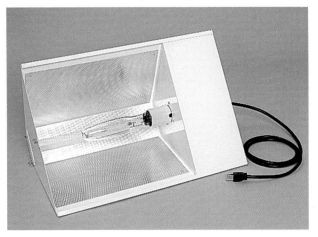

WATER, WATER

A good water supply is another essential component for a successful home greenhouse. While water can be supplied with a garden hose or even from a rain barrel, having it piped into the greenhouse is by far the most convenient and efficient arrangement.

PLUMBING

You can easily extend home water lines to an attached or freestanding greenhouse; in cold climates they must be underneath the frost line. Water may also be pumped from a rain barrel or a well near or under the greenhouse.

Ideally, the greenhouse should have a sink or tub with both hot and cold water and a threaded mixing faucet. Most plants prefer to be watered with tepid rather than cold water and hot water facilitates greenhouse cleanup. A separate threaded cold water spigot can supply water for an automatic drip system or a humidifier. Any plumbing lines connected to the house system must incorporate a backflow device to prevent any chemicals (from an integrated fertilizer, for instance) entering the house water system.

KEEPING PLANTS WET

While some greenhouse owners prefer to use a watering can, it is easier and quicker to use a small hose with a watering wand. A lightweight, self-storing hose that recoils is most convenient. Wands for both misting and watering are available.

AUTOMATIC WATERING SYSTEMS

Some gardeners prefer not to provide overhead water to their plants as constant moisture on foliage can encourage diseases. However, if you provide good air circulation and

AUTOMATIC SPRAYERS

Irrigation systems can be much like those used outdoors, with spray heads that can be connected to risers. Use an automatic timer to deliver consistent amounts of water.

MISTING SYSTEMS

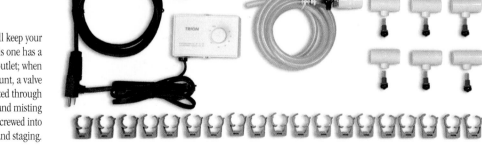

A fully equipped misting system will keep your plants healthy and happily growing. This one has a humidistat that plugs into a 120-volt outlet; when the humidity drops below a set amount, a valve activates the water flow. Water is directed through a filter and pressure gauge to PVC pipes and misting nozzles. The grey pipe hangers can be screwed into aluminum or wood framing and staging.

work with healthy plant material, it is unlikely that regular overhead watering will cause problems. The most common type of irrigation system includes a water filter, valves, tubing or pipes, risers, nozzles, and an electronic timer. There are a wide variety of riser and nozzle combinations; the simplest setup includes risers set at mid-bench, with a full-circle spray pattern.

Drip irrigation delivers water to plants one drop at a time. In a simple drip-irrigation system water is conveyed around the greenhouse in flexible tubing. Small drippers are attached to the supply line and positioned over the plants. The system is usually controlled by a standard watering timer or may be activated from a control panel.

MISTING

Misting systems provide needed humidity, especially for cuttings and for tropical plants that like a humid environment. A good misting system can cool the greenhouse by 10 to 20°F during the hot months. However, you should only run the system during the day, because dampness at night can encourage plant diseases. Small greenhouse humidifiers, some of which can be plumbed directly into the water-supply line, can provide mist for a small area. A simple misting system, similar to a drip-irrigation system, uses emitters rather than drippers. More-sophisticated misting systems can fill the greenhouse with fine mist or fog. Both humidifiers and misting systems can be controlled by a humidistat, which activates the system when the humidity levels drop below a set point.

Some humidifiers can be connected to a garden hose to maintain a constant water supply, especially for seedlings or tropical plants, both of which benefit from high humidity.

CAPILLARY WATERING

In capillary watering, plants are placed on a wet material, and moisture is drawn up into the pot by "capillary action"—the principle that water rises through a porous substance. You can also create capillary action by placing a wick between the growing medium in the pot and a water source. The plant draws only as much moisture as it needs. Benches of wet sand were the traditional method, but most capillary watering systems now use a feltlike mat of synthetic fiber. The mat should be placed on a sheet of polyethylene film covering a raised surface or tray that is flat and level. One end of the mat should be dipped into a water reservoir (right).

CAPILLARY WATERING

Water is wicked up to plant roots

Reservoir

Capillary matting

WATER QUALITY

Hard water can leave unsightly deposits on plant leaves, but water that has been passed through a softening system should not be used on plants because of its high salt content. If your plants are showing signs of mineral deposits, you can install a reverse osmosis water system that removes all dissolved solids by passing the water through a filter under pressure. It takes 4 to 11 gallons of water to produce one gallon of pure water, but the wastewater can subsequently be used for outdoor irrigation.

INTERIOR DETAILS

"Staging" refers to the plant benches or tables that usually line the interior walls of the greenhouse. Very wide greenhouses may have an additional center row of benches. Arranging benches in a "T" formation can expand the growing space. You can also install portable benches below the tables and move them into the aisles when more light is needed.

You can make simple benches with concrete blocks, which also act as heat sinks, or with moisture-resistant wooden or PVC frames. All benches can be topped with wooden slats or mesh screens that drain well. Premanufactured greenhouse benches are usually made of aluminum or wood and are often topped with metal mesh screening, slats, or plastic grid panels. (A water-permeable weed barrier material on top of the benches can catch falling debris and keep it off the greenhouse floor.) The tops of potting and propagating benches have a deep solid tray to hold the growing medium.

You can create more growing space with freestanding tiered shelving units that resemble steps. Access to each plant is easy, and all plants receive full light. Unless you plan to water with a watering can, do not build or place benches against a greenhouse knee wall. Watering with a hose will result in excess moisture on the interior of the knee wall and a subsequent buildup of algae. Likewise, to avoid condensation and rot don't position benches directly against wooden walls.

SHELVES

In many greenhouses you can attach shelves to the wall framing. These shelves may be glass, plastic, or metal. Lean-to greenhouses have a solid wall to which you can also secure shelving. The popular painted or plastic-coated wire closet shelves work well; you can anchor them to the wall with brackets.

HANGING PLANTS

If the ridgepole or roof framing is strong enough, you can suspend plants from purpose-made metal hooks that fit into aluminum extrusions, or from hooks screwed into wooden rafters. You can also hang containers from a long pole suspended horizontally above the benches. Small hanging plants can be suspended from strips of wire dangling from the shelves. But remember that hanging pots will cast shade and drip water on plants below.

The owner of this greenhouse has found a way to maximize its growing space. Potted plants line the benches and fit snugly on the floor underneath. Grapevines clamber up support pipes, from which hanging plants are suspended.

USING SPACE EFFECTIVELY

Set up the interior of your greenhouse so that it is comfortable for you to move around in, and also so that your plants receive the benefits of any microclimates within the greenhouse. For instance, it's wise to place taller plants on the north side of the structure, where they will cast less shadow on smaller plants. Don't feel confined to the conventional system of a U-shaped or single-aisle layout. Instead, draw various layouts on graph paper to see which arrangement will work best. And if space permits, don't forget to include a quiet spot with a comfortable chair.

GLAZING
The hottest parts of the greenhouse are near the glazing, especially in the top half of the space and on the south side. Lower areas of the greenhouse and the north-facing spaces are cooler. However, in cold-winter regions, any spot near the glazing will be cooler during winter.

STORAGE
Use the area underneath your benches for storage, or bring in a storage bench for double-duty seating and storage. Raise bags of material up onto bricks or planks so they don't get wet, or place them in plastic buckets. Any chemicals and sharp tools, of course, should be kept in a locked cabinet or box.

HEATERS
Plants that love warmth can be set near the heater. But some plants are intolerant of the drafts and temperature changes that are more pronounced immediately around the heaters and exhaust fans.

SPACING
Good air circulation is critical. Don't overcrowd your plants.

TRELLISES
Those that run north-south receive the most even distribution of light.

REFLECTION
Paint surfaces inside the greenhouse white to enhance light reflection within the structure.

WATER
Drains should be set near the center of the floor or near the water source. The floor must slope slightly down toward the drain.

SHELVING
The upper shelves will be warmer and lighter, so raise up your tropicals to ceiling height. Don't let them come into direct contact with the glazing, however, and make sure they receive plenty of water.

BENCHES
In addition to traditional benches, you can install stepped benches, which display a greater number of plants. Typical greenhouse benches are 30 to 36 inches high.

BEDS
Those against the walls should be no wider than 3 feet to allow access. Those in the center can be 5 or 6 feet wide.

VEGETABLES
Place your frequently harvested herbs and vegetables where they are most accessible. Remember that mixed plantings provide better protection against pests and diseases.

SHADE
The shady, cooler areas under benches can also be used to grow shade-loving plants. If your preference is for light-lovers, you can install supplemental lights underneath the benches.

WALKWAYS
No more than 25 percent of your greenhouse floor space should be devoted to walkways. Two-foot-wide aisles are adequate for pedestrians; 4 feet is required for comfortable passage of a wheelchair.

GARDEN ROOMS

The fashion for attaching glass structures to the main house began in Victorian England where "orangeries," as they were called, provided temperate growing conditions for oranges and other such tender plants from milder climates. Many of today's conservatories still emulate this 19th-century model, incorporating ornate metal framing, elaborate columns, and even special touches such as cupolas, copper trim, gables, and stained glass.

In more modern times, the concept of a sunroom or solarium has expanded to mean any sun-filled room in the house—whether a sitting room, an indoor-outdoor eating area, or even a place to put a spa or a koi pond.

Select plants for your conservatory based on how you'll use the space, its size, and the amount of available light. Generally, orchids, dwarf citrus trees, and other flowering houseplants have high light requirements. Ferns, dracaena, bromeliads, and non-flowering houseplants will thrive in lower light levels. To grow cactus and other desert plants, your conservatory atmosphere will need to mimic the environment native to these plants—warm and dry.

A snowbound conservatory in New York state doubles as a growing space and an artist's studio.

RIGHT: The curved glass eaves in this modern sunroom provide optimal light for plants. Although this comfortable space is primarily a breakfast or coffee nook, supports attached to the framing members allow vines to clamber overhead.

BELOW: Beautifully framed and outfitted, this classic brick-floored structure could serve as a living or entertaining space. Benches loaded with flowering plants, however, suggest that it is being used exclusively for horticulture. Rare is the greenhouse gardener who complains of empty space.

CONSERVATORY OR GREENHOUSE?

Greenhouses and conservatories share many common features—walls and ceilings of glass or plastic glazing, lots of light, and plant-filled spaces—yet they have one important difference. A greenhouse is designed to create the best conditions for plants, whereas a conservatory is meant to provide comfortable surroundings primarily for its human inhabitants.

This means that a conservatory must be maintained at room temperature and that the humidity must not be excessive, yet there must also be sufficient moisture and air movement to accommodate the types of plants you wish to grow. Although the basic environment of the conservatory is determined by the heating and cooling system, you can incorporate greenhouse accessories such as fans, vents, and humidifiers to provide optimum growing conditions for plants.

A conservatory can be designed as part of the original house plan, it can be added as an extra room, or it can even be freestanding—there's no rule that a conservatory must be attached to the house. As with other garden structures, the primary design consideration should be how well the room's appearance will fit in with the existing architecture and with the garden. In any case, as a full-fledged house addition, a conservatory must be designed and built by a professional, it must meet all local building codes, and it is likely to cost significantly more than a simple greenhouse. It's also likely, however, to increase your home's value.

A true working greenhouse can be attached to the main house. This arched entryway, filled with potted plants, provides a gracious transition between the two rooms.

Detached from the house yet blended into the garden and surrounded by flower beds, this brick knee-walled glass house could serve as either a conservatory or a true propagation and growing house.

Traditional framing, patterned water-resistant flooring, and indoor-outdoor furniture tell you this is a conservatory. The room feels enveloped by the greenery outdoors; tender plants such as flowering maple and geraniums also bloom continuously within.

SUN SPACES

Although the distinction between a greenhouse and a conservatory is clear, the difference between a conservatory and a sunroom or solarium is not quite as obvious. In fact, these terms are used interchangeably, and all are variations on the same theme: a room that can accommodate plants as well as people.

There are many ways to bring more light into an existing room. Installing full or partial glazing on the ceiling or walls, or even adding extra windows and skylights, brightens up a room enough to allow plants to flourish. In summer, the glazing panels may be used interchangeably with screens. You can modify an existing porch or patio with a prefabricated or custom sunroom kit, as long as there is sufficient underpinning to support the structure, and the floor can be made waterproof. The same orientation considerations apply to a sunroom as with a lean-to greenhouse—south-facing is best. If temperatures drop below 55°F, a small portable heater will raise the temperature.

A solarium is a cross between a garden room and a greenhouse, but the emphasis is on plant display. Solariums are usually on upper floors and are built with glazed walls and at least a partially glazed roof.

If you can't afford the time, space, or money to invest in a sunroom or solarium, consider transforming a porch, an atrium, a bay window, or part of an indoor living area into garden room. The humidity and oxygenated air provided by the plants can create a beneficial ambience and microclimate.

Container-grown plants do best, and are easiest to water, when they are grouped together rather than scattered. Place containers in saucers, or make a platform of bricks or concrete pavers on a heavy plastic sheet to protect the floor. Add some garden art or a small water feature for accent and interest. To further increase humidity levels, place pebbles or decorative glass in plant saucers and mist the plants with water every day.

Portable garden carts, shelves, or lighted display cases, sometimes in bookcases, can house small indoor display gardens or propagation units. You can usually supply enough light with fixtures fitted with greenhouse bulbs (page 41). Another option is to install a skylight within the entrance to your home and create a dramatic atrium that you fill with unusual or sculptural plants and statuary.

FACING PAGE, TOP: Even during a cold Virginia winter, this sunroom has just the right conditions for a wide range of tender plants, tropicals, roses, orchids, and even succulents.

BOTTOM: A conservatory corner is filled with an arrangement of containers, such as a raised "window box."

This space provides the light-filled conditions that plants love, along with comfortable seating and exterior views for its inhabitants. By painting the interior woodwork white, the owners increased the amount of reflected sunlight.

A tiered plant stand, an elegant statue, and some climbing ivy—that's all it took to transform these French doors into the background for an indoor garden.

Ceiling-to-floor wall glazing allows in the most light, but if you have several house walls in the garden room, a glazed ceiling or skylights can boost light levels considerably.

BUILDING CONSIDERATIONS

A conservatory is a major addition to your home and it's worth spending the time and money to have the work properly done. Your first decision is how you will approach the design and construction.

You can have an architect design the structure and then hire a contractor to build it. This ensures that you have control over the design. Some companies offer custom designs (page 19); you can also purchase a preassembled model that is delivered to you for construction. In many cases it's best to work with the company's own assembly team, but you often have the option of hiring a local builder or contractor to do the work. Whatever you decide, you must get building approval from your local planning commission before you start the project.

First, decide where you'd like the structure to go. South-facing is best for overall lighting; east-facing structures receive the best morning light. Then you'll need to decide how the conservatory will be connected to the house and what kind of foundation it requires. Ceiling-to-floor glazing allows in the most light, but a knee wall (page 25) may better match your home's architecture and provides an easy place to conceal utility lines. It's relatively simple to tie into house plumbing and electrical systems, but if you install a pool or water feature you may require an additional water heater.

Framing will either be wood or metal. Wood must be building-grade, and where it will be exposed, it's best to use treated lumber or naturally rot-resistant cedar or redwood to resist moisture. Aluminum and steel can both be coated with a variety of colors. Because metal conducts cold, these frames may have thermal breaks (page 30) to help prevent condensation caused by varying temperatures.

Your choice of glazing is critical, and it's common to use different types of glass on the structure. Tempered glass is strongest and resists breakage from hail, earth movement, and debris—it's a good choice for the ceiling or skylights if you live in an area prone to storms. Insulated glass is often used in colder climates or for doors, where condensation is likely to occur. Tinted glass can reduce heat and glare if your conservatory is exposed to direct sunlight or your climate is very hot. Curved-glass eaves provide a traditional look.

Finally, think about the flooring. Waterproof ceramic or synthetic tile, brick, and stone are all good choices, as is wood, which can be treated to resist water. Again, it depends on your preferences and the style of your house.

Beyond these basics lie endless variations. You may choose water features, built-in beds or window seats, fancy finials, sliding glass panels, special lighting, or other embellishments.

Most conservatories require the help of a designer and this one in Maryland is no exception. By working with the owner and the garden designer, not only was the structure built to match the home's architecture, but it was beautifully integrated with the garden. A path of stone steps leads toward the doorway and generous plantings surround both path and conservatory.

WHAT ARE YOUR OPTIONS?

❧ Will it be attached to the house or freestanding?

❧ What kind of access should there be to a house-attached model, both from adjoining rooms and out to the garden? You can choose between French doors, sliding doors, or even no door.

❧ Exposure to light is important for plant growth (page 21). South- and east-facing orientations are usually best.

❧ The foundation will be specified by local building codes, depending on the frost line. Consider knee walls that tie into the foundation.

❧ Framing may be moisture-resistant wood, aluminum, or steel.

❧ Choices in glazing include tempered, curved, tinted, or insulated glass (page 31).

❧ Windows may be fixed or hand-operated casements. In areas where insects are a problem, any operable windows should be screened.

❧ Vents are usually positioned in the same manner as a larger greenhouse (page 33) and can be controlled with a temperature sensor.

❧ Fans can keep air circulating and cool things down.

❧ Flooring should be waterproof and match your home's interior. Add rugs to seating areas for warmth, but never carpet a conservatory.

❧ You may install raised growing beds, or you can rely on containers to house your plants.

❧ The conservatory can be a wet environment. Electrical connections ideally should be GFCI protected. Extra circuits may have to be added at the house panel, and should be installed by an electrician.

❧ Watering in conservatories is often done by hand, but you can install misting or drip irrigation systems similar to those used in greenhouses (page 43). To increase humidity, set plants on trays of pebbles, mist frequently, and use portable humidifiers.

❧ Floor drains may be necessary if you are growing tropical plants or have a spa or pool.

❧ Drainage from condensation and irrigation must be carried away; a common method is via an interior gutter system.

❧ Water features (page 54) increase humidity and are well-suited to tropical plantings.

❧ Shade cloth or even sheer interior curtains can cool down the conservatory when temperatures soar outside.

❧ The heating service is likely to depend on your house system. For the benefit of your plants, ask your architect or builder which type of locally available heating system will be least likely to dry the atmosphere. If the rest of your house calls for air conditioning, then your conservatory will, too.

❧ Natural light is best, of course, but you may need supplemental lighting if your conservatory is shaded or has a northern exposure. For evening lighting, floor lamps enhance the coziness of your indoor garden.

A stately structure for a gracious garden.

ABOVE RIGHT: It may be cold and rainy outdoors on Bainbridge Island, Washington, but indoors the bougainvillea are blooming. This conservatory pond measures 9 feet by 16 feet, is two feet deep, and is sealed with a rubber pool liner. In the water, tropical water lilies, thalia, and floating water hyacinths are thriving. Around the room are containers filled with angel's trumpet, ferns, orchids, and passion vine. Goldfish keep insects at bay.

ABOVE: An indoor water feature can be as simple as a store-bought fountain, which requires only a small submersible pump and an electrical outlet. Or, you can install a full-size fountain and surround it with greenery.

INTERIOR WATER FEATURES

If you are creating an indoor garden, there's a good chance you'll want a water feature. The popularity of water gardening has ensured that you have a wide range of choice in portable fountains and small-scale ponds. But if you want a larger or more permanent installation, you'll have to consult an architect or builder.

The ease with which you can build an indoor pond depends a great deal on your climate. Those in temperate regions have the luxury of constructing indoor-outdoor waterways that flow into the garden proper. In cold-winter climates, however, you'll have to keep all the water indoors. You'll also have to consider the structural underpinning of your flooring and the depth of the frost line in your region.

PONDS

You can create a small pond anywhere in the conservatory simply by filling a large ceramic vase or waterproofed barrel with water and adding some water plants or even a fish or two. Raised-bed ponds are another option; they must be carefully lined, preferably with a molded plastic liner that resists tearing. You'll need to support the lining with a few inches of sand.

A pond whose surface is flush with the floor level calls for greater preparation and more careful design. Don't try to install a below-floor pond without first consulting a building professional and a water-gardening specialist.

First of all, you must be sure that the room's support members can bear the weight of the pond when it is filled with water—building codes specify the load a floor can withstand. (For each foot of water, estimate 62 lbs. per square foot of floor space.) Also verify that there are not likely to be problems with the ground temperature—it may be that you'll need to insulate the pond to prevent dramatic temperature swings. You'll want to have a good water-input and filtration system, as well as a means by which to drain the pond. If you plan to have plants and fish in the pond, lighting is essential, and it should mimic sunlight as much as possible; you may need to supplement with fluorescent or full-spectrum bulbs.

Moving water not only sounds delightful but also generates more air moisture. A recirculating waterfall doesn't require any connection to a plumbing outlet; it need only be kept topped up with water. Most important is that you use a waterproof liner or seal to ensure that moisture does not leak from the waterway.

FISH

An indoor pond can support fish, but unlike an outdoor pond, it cannot establish a self-sustaining ecosystem. To keep the pond clear, you'll need a foam or biological filter system that circulates the entire water volume once per hour. Have your house water supply tested for chemicals such as chlorine, chloramine, fluoride, and iron, which can all be harmful to aquatic life. Unlike those in an outdoor pond, where insects usually provide plenty of food, fish indoors require feeding.

Protect fish from the household cat, and be aware that koi can sometimes jump out of the pond—you don't want to find them on the conservatory floor. Provide as much light as possible for ten hours a day; if there is insufficient daylight, then install full-spectrum lighting (page 40).

You'll need to monitor the temperature, the pH, and the ammonia and nitrogen levels of your pond water, and adjust them if necessary with products that are available at pond-supply stores and garden centers. Replace the water once a year, and remove debris from the pond monthly.

The koi in this indoor-outdoor pond have learned to recognize their owner's presence; they know it signifies food. With plenty of space, some may grow to more than 18 inches in length.

RECIPE FOR A SMALL POND

To prevent the growth of algae, you should aim to keep at least two-thirds of the water surface covered with plants. The basic recommended mix of plants for a small indoor pond is:

∾ **Water lilies**, hardy or tropical, and lotus. Divide these every few years.

∾ **Floating plants**, such as water hyacinth, water lettuce, and duckweed. Skim duckweed off the surface if the pond becomes more than 75 percent covered.

∾ **Oxygenating plants**, such as parrot's feather and milfoil. These can quickly multiply and will need to be periodically thinned out.

∾ **Bog, or marginal, plants**, which can include rushes and reeds, acorus, canna, dwarf horsetail, lobelia, cattails, and irises. Keep these in containers to prevent them from overcrowding the pond.

CONSERVATORY PLANTS

Keep in mind that the more extras you include—water features, specimen plants, and other items—the more work your conservatory will require. If you'd prefer to have your plants merely as decoration, use large, slow-growing container plants that require minimal maintenance.

Outdoors a magnolia heralds spring, but indoors it's always summer. A magnificent and soaring space such as this can house a wide and lush array of plants. Included are orchids, hanging sedums, and palms.

For a lusher conservatory, consider the space as a work in progress. Begin by growing some common houseplants such as ferns, *Spathiphyllum*, dieffenbachia, *Ficus*, and coleus. Once you get a feel for your conservatory's light, temperature, and humidity levels, move on to slightly more specialized plants. Try bougainvillea, gardenia, orchids, and even tree ferns if space permits. If your conservatory isn't bursting with plants during the first year, don't worry. Just like any garden, the conservatory grows and matures with age.

Many palms, trees, and vines will grow quickly in the near-perfect conditions the conservatory provides, and they will soon be nearing the roof line. Rather than putting them in growing beds, try planting these fast-growing items in containers to limit their growth.

GROWING CONDITIONS

Conservatories are designed to provide more light than is available in a typical room in your home, so expect all your plants to grow more quickly than regular houseplants. But because many plants have specific light requirements in order to flower, you need to observe the intensity and duration of the light and how it changes during the year.

Warm conservatories (60°F and above) offer an environment where lush tropical plants can thrive, while cooler spaces (40–59°F) are appropriate for camellias and similar cool-condition plants. Some plants, such as daphne, need cooler conditions in order to set buds.

Humidity levels and available water will also influence your choices. Fast-growing tropicals need lots of water and high humidity. Some, including tree ferns, need to stay moist constantly and require frequent dousings with water. This means having a constant supply of water and a proper drainage system. You are much more likely to water if there's a tap close at hand.

Whatever you decide to grow in your conservatory, remember that you'll have to care for the plants and maintain the conservatory with as much care as if you were using the space for propagating plants. Follow the cleaning and maintenance tips described on page 86. Also, watch for insect and disease outbreaks prompted by the warm and humid conditions.

A SAMPLE OF CONSERVATORY FAVORITES

PLANT NAME	TEMP. RANGE (°F) (MIN/MAX)	HUMIDITY/ NOTES
Light Needs—High		
Acacia	40 or lower/60–80	
Agave	40/60–85	Very high light
Begonia	55/60–80	
Billbergia	45/60–85	
Bougainvillea	45/60–90	High light for flowering
Brugmansia	40/60–85	
Calla lily	40/60–90	
Camellia japonica	40/60–65	
Canna	55/80–95	Store rhizomes
Citrus	40–50/60–90	
Clivia	40/60–85	
Fuchsia	25–40/75	High humidity
Gardenia	60–85	High humidity
Hibiscus	55/60–85	
Jasmine	45/60–90	
Kalanchoe	50/60–85	
Nephrolepis	50/75	High humidity
Norfolk Island pine	40/80	
Passionflower vine	40/60–85	
Pelargonium	45/70–75	
Light Needs—Medium to High		
Aechma	50/60–85	
Allamanda	55/60–85	High humidity
Clerodendrun	55/60–85	
Cordyline	50–65 /80	Med. to very high light, depending on spp.
Cycads	50/60–80	
Guzmania	60/65–85	High humidity
Hoya	45/60–85	High humidity
Lotus berthelotti	45–50/60–85	
Mandevilla	40/60–85	High humidity
Musa	55/60–90	High humidity
Plumeria	65/70–85	High humidity
Pomegranate	45/60–90	
Rhododendron spp.	45 to flower/60–70	
Staghorn fern	50/60–85	High humidity
Stephanotis	50/60–90	
Strelitzia	55/60–80	Avoid hot summers
Strobilanthes	50/60–90	
Tibouchina	50/60–80	High humidity

CLOCKWISE FROM TOP LEFT: Brugmansia, begonia, ivy, azalea

PLANT NAME	TEMP. RANGE (°F) (MIN/MAX)	HUMIDITY/ NOTES
Light Needs—Medium		
Asplenium	50/60–85	
Dieffenbachia	65–70/75–80	
Dracaena	65–70/75–80	
Ficus	50/60–80	High humidity
Sansevieria	65–75/75–80	
Schefflera	60/85	
Light Needs—Low to Medium		
Dicksonia (tree ferns)	45/60–80	Keep moist/Low to high light, depending on season
Ivy	36–40/50–70	High humidity
Monstera	50/60–90	High humidity/Good light in winter

GROWING YOUR OWN

Which is better: starting from seed, cuttings, or nursery plants? The answer depends on your timing, patience, and budget.

	SEEDS	CUTTINGS	BUYING PLANTS
TIME	Longest time to produce flowers and fruit. Easiest with annual plants, such as many vegetables; can have seedlings for planting out in a few weeks.	Cuttings take less time to reach maturity, but some require several months to establish a good root system. Best for most perennials and many woody plants.	Plants are immediately ready for planting. Those in smaller containers often offer best value, as they quickly catch up in size when planted.
SEASON	Seeds can be started anytime, but must be timed for planting-out date.	Availability of cuttings limited to certain seasons.	Availability of plants limited to certain seasons.
EXPENSE	Seeds are generally inexpensive.	Cuttings free if they come from your own stock.	Most expensive option.
QUANTITY	Seeds produce greater quantity in smaller space.	Quantity depends on plants available for cutting.	Price may limit quantities.
EQUIPMENT	Growing medium. Starting trays and pots. Large containers or built-in beds if remaining indoors.	Growing medium and rooting hormone. Starting pots. Large containers or built-in beds if remaining indoors.	Large containers or built-in beds if remaining in greenhouse.
SUCCESS RATE	Rate varies with seed type, and depends on proper storage and culture. Seedlings can suffer from damping off; it's best to sow more than needed.	Rate depends on plant type, time of year, and careful culture. Again, it's best to take more cuttings than needed.	Rate depends on quality of plants purchased. Shop at reliable nurseries that guarantee their products.
SPECIAL NOTES	You have greatest choice of species and varieties. Some seeds require special procedures to initiate germination.	You can choose plants with desirable characteristics. You can collect and propagate specimens from friends or plant clubs.	You can quickly obtain specific plants You can be sure of a plant's appearance before purchase.

Planting from seed results in large numbers of identical plants.

Woody plants and perennials can be propagated from cuttings.

Purchasing plants from the nursery is the most expensive option.

A YEAR INDOORS

Your regular greenhouse tasks will depend on the seasons, the climate, the equipment you have, and whether you use the greenhouse for propagation or for specimen plants. This guide will tell you what to expect. Specialty plants, such as orchids, have their own requirements.

MID- TO LATE WINTER Bring bulb containers out of cold storage and into the greenhouse to force them (page 73). Check tubers or bulbs you have in storage to ensure that no diseases have taken hold.

Sow annual seeds, such as pansies and primroses, that require cool temperatures or are slow to germinate. This is also a good time to start tomatoes for greenhouse beds you'll plant in midspring. Continue to start cool-season greenhouse crops such as lettuce, leafy greens, and peas. Apply a dilute water-soluble fertilizer as seedlings grow.

Take cuttings of zonal pelargoniums, fuchsias, and geraniums you brought in last year. Pot up the cuttings when their roots develop. Prune grapes.

In the conservatory, cut back climbing plants and vines to keep growth under control. Make the cut just one or two buds above the beginning of last year's growth. Deadhead early-blooming plants such as azaleas and cyclamens. Leave bulb foliage on plants until it browns.

On the occasional bright, warm day, ventilate the greenhouse, but don't allow the interior temperature to drop.

Order seeds and equipment for the coming year, and plan your growing schedule now.

EARLY SPRING TO MIDSPRING Continue to sow seeds of greenhouse vegetable crops such as tomatoes, peppers, beans, and cucumbers. Sow seeds for those annuals that tolerate some cold weather, such as sweet alyssum and snapdragons. Prepare greenhouse beds for late-winter tomato seeds, and transplant seedlings in midspring.

Take cuttings of coleus, chrysanthemums, and pelargoniums. Root them at temperatures between 50°F and 61°F. Propagate dahlias by potting up tubers.

Seedings grown in peat pots are ready to plant out in late spring.

The greenhouse can heat up quickly in spring's bright sunshine. Apply a light coat of shade paint to the glass, especially over areas near sensitive tropical plants. By midspring, you should apply another layer of shade paint or have a shading system up and running (page 34). Ventilation is critical at this time because the greenhouse warms and cools quickly with changing cloud cover (page 32).

Maintain constant soil moisture for young plants. You may need to water more than once a day because of midspring's increasing sunlight and temperatures.

Fertilize citrus, grapes, and other fruits starting to push out buds now.

Prepare the soil in your outside vegetable garden; then sow tomato, corn, melon and cucumber seeds. When all danger of frost has passed, move out tender plants that were overwintered indoors.

LATE SPRING TO SUMMER In late spring, use a cold frame to harden off these annuals you had previously sown in midspring.

Plant vegetable seedlings into greenhouse beds in late spring and start training these crops around supports. Pinch tomato side shoots and fertilize every week once fruits swell. Thin heavily bearing fruits such as grapes. Transfer melons sown in midspring to a cold frame for hardening off. Plant cucumbers in growing bags.

Provide shade for flowering plants and increase humidity, making sure there is plenty of ventilation and airflow. Fertilize fast-growing plants weekly.

In early summer, make room in the greenhouse by moving plants that have finished flowering into the garden. Frequently deadhead the plants that remain inside to prevent clutter and disease.

Your greenhouse plants need lots of watering now. Terra-cotta pots dry out quickly, as do large-leafed plants. If you do not have an automatic misting system (page 42), keep humidity high and plants cool by hosing down the floors and spritzing the leaves with water. Depending on your climate, you may need to ventilate the greenhouse on warm nights.

Pot Cape primrose *(Streptocarpus)* seedlings sown in winter, and sow another batch of seeds for flowering later in the year. Propagate African violets and rex begonias with leaf cuttings in early summer (page 72).

Many insects emerge in early summer. When temperatures remain warm enough for plants to spend a night outside, empty the greenhouse for a thorough cleaning (page 88). Protect your plants during their night outside with a row cover or sheet.

MID- TO LATE SUMMER Midsummer greenhouse conditions vary greatly depending on your location. In areas with only mild humidity, water your plants at least once every day to prevent wilting and plant stress. "Damp down" shelves and floors with water. If you live in a very hot, arid climate and do not have an evaporative cooling system, simple shading and ventilation may not be enough to keep your greenhouse cool, so its use during the summer will be limited.

Propagate plants from softwood cuttings at this time for a new crop of plants for the following growing season. Good candidates include poinsettia, lavender, and buddleia.

Continue to take regal and zonal pelargonium and fuchsia cuttings through late summer. Start potting up your rooted poinsettia cuttings.

Tomato and cucumber plants should be producing fruit. If roots appear on the soil surface, add a layer of compost as a topdressing. Keep the plants well watered but do not overwater.

In warm climates, sow seeds of cool-season crops for transplanting to the garden in fall. Plant fall-flowering bulbs in containers.

Reapply shade paint to glass where it has worn off. If the greenhouse needs painting, late summer is the best time.

Divide lily bulbs in fall.

Also complete any repairs—broken glass panes, loose caulking, and torn plastic. Make sure the greenhouse's vents close properly and the heating system is in tip-top shape before the first cold snap hits.

EARLY FALL TO MIDFALL Sow seeds of colorful spring annuals for next year. Keep the greenhouse temperature cool, between 55 and 61°F. Continue to take cuttings of pelargoniums, impatiens, and other tender perennials you would like to save for next year.

Prepare for next spring's bulb crop by potting each of your favorite bulbs at least twice as deep as the bulb's width. Keep the pots in a dark, cool spot for eight weeks. Divide lily bulbs by scaling (page 73).

Remove most of the shade paint or cloth from the greenhouse, but provide some shade for tender seedlings and new cuttings on sunny autumn days.

Keep poinsettias away from artificial night lighting, which will disturb their coloring process.

Water less frequently in early fall and midfall. Too much water encourages disease.

Prepare for winter if you are in a cold climate. Clean glass panes and cover them with plastic sheeting or a layer of plastic bubble wrap. This forms an energy-conserving layer of insulating air. Cover ventilators with separate sheets of plastic.

Bring in frost-tender plants.

LATE FALL TO EARLY WINTER During damp weather, keep vents closed. Open them only on warm, sunny mornings or afternoons.

Pot up fall-sown annuals and any rooted cuttings in small containers. Store fuchsias, begonias, and other plants that require a dormant period in a cool area of the greenhouse. Water these plants periodically until spring.

Stop fertilizing poinsettias and let the soil dry slightly. This hardens the plant and allows a longer color period.

Find a warm spot for plants that bloom in late winter to encourage flowering. To delay blooming, place plants in a cooler location. Plants in flower need more regular watering than those that are dormant or not flowering.

Clockwise from upper right: self-watering tray; compressed peat cubes; square pots; cell packs; peat pots; growing cells.

KEEP IT MOIST

Watering a seed tray from above may splash soil and disturb seeds, so it's best to provide consistent moisture from below. To bottom-water your seeds, simply place the seed flat in a larger container partly filled with water. The growing mix will absorb water evenly through the drainage holes. Remove the water tray when the mix is saturated.

You can also use a self-watering seed-starting system (below), which has seed cells atop a woven fabric that wicks water from a reservoir. You need only to keep the reservoir topped up with water. But don't overfill—sodden matting can promote algae.

Some seed-starting trays have domed lids to increase humidity levels. You can create a similar effect using upside-down plastic sweater boxes or clear-lidded aluminum bakery trays with drainage holes poked in the bottom. But beware—covering the seedlings can also encourage fungal growth, so remove lids as soon as seedlings emerge. If you are propagating large numbers of plants, consider a misting system that can deliver a controlled amount of moisture (page 42).

EQUIPMENT AND SUPPLIES

You can find basic propagation supplies at your local nursery or garden center. Mail-order companies offer specialty items such as self-watering seed-starting systems and newspaper-pot and soil-cube makers (page 110). Whatever your personal preferences, containers should be durable and spacious enough to accommodate the plants you intend to grow.

CONTAINERS

Shallow plastic flats measuring 10 by 20 inches offer space for hundreds of seeds and cuttings. Smaller packs are typically made of plastic or pressed wood fiber. For starting just a few plants, square pots are most space-efficient. Many gardeners prefer the look of terra-cotta and clay, but these materials are fragile and porous, which means the potting mix can quickly dry out. Glazed pots or those with ceramic sealer retain moisture longer.

Peat pots and compressed peat pellets also dry out rapidly, but they have the advantage of being ready for direct transplanting to a larger pot or into the ground outside. The same is true of newspaper pots or compressed soil cubes, which are formed by hand with a press.

Cell packs are clusters of lightweight plastic pots that keep plant roots separate. They're easy to carry and they save space. If you are propagating seeds or cuttings of perennials, trees, shrubs, and plants with taproots, use a "plug" tray with cells 4 or more inches deep—they promote strong root growth.

Before using containers, wash them with a solution of 1 part bleach to 10 parts water. A child's wading pool or a bathtub is an ideal place to clean large numbers of pots simultaneously.

BOTTOM HEAT

Seeds and cuttings need moisture and constant warmth to germinate and root successfully. But moist growing mix tends to cool plants and slow their growth, and even with careful venting, the temperature inside the greenhouse fluctuates. You can employ heating coils, cables, and mats to keep the mix sufficiently warm.

Loop cables back and forth along a bench, making sure they don't touch but remain 3 to 4 inches apart. Cover the cables with at least 1 inch of sand to provide a

buffer between the cables and the seed-starting containers. An easier option is to place a heating mat on the potting bench (left). For best results, set the thermostat at the ideal germination or rooting temperature for your plants. Most seeds and cuttings require temperatures between 70 and 75°F, but some need temperatures as low as 65°F.

GROWING MIXES

The basic function of germination and growing mixes is to provide a foundation for the developing plant. A light, porous mix allows easy penetration and airflow that encourage a healthy root system. For seeds, a uniform texture is best; you may need to screen the mix to eliminate oversize particles and debris.

You'll find a wide range of germination and growing mixes at nurseries and garden centers. Most contain vermiculite and perlite (expanded micaceous and volcanic materials, respectively), as well as sand, shredded bark, sphagnum and peat mosses, and other organic materials. Buy only mixes presterilized to kill soil-borne pathogens, insect eggs, and weed seeds. Never use regular garden soil or even commercial outdoor or container planting mixes for starting plants.

Most growing mixes also include nutrients that encourage plant growth, and have a neutral pH (7), rather than one that is acidic or alkaline. The pH doesn't directly affect plant growth, but it does influence the amounts and types of nutrients available to the plant. As you gain experience, you may find that mixing your own recipes is best. You can make small batches to ensure that the mix is fresh, and you can vary its texture and structure for different purposes. Cacti, African violets, orchids, and other specialty plants require specific components and pH values.

The quality of the water in your greenhouse is also important. Minerals such as sodium, calcium, and magnesium can affect the growing plants. Municipal water with added fluoride can damage leaves, and well, lake, or river water may contain algae seeds, excess salts, or even chemical contaminants. Likewise, softened water is less than ideal for plants because of its high salt content. If your plants seem to be suffering from an otherwise inexplicable decline, burned leaves, or waterlogging, contact your local Cooperative Extension Office or a diagnostic lab to test your greenhouse's water supply.

MIXING AND STERILIZING SOIL

If you're making your own starting mix, experiment with variations on a basic recipe of 14 parts sphagnum, 3 parts perlite, 3 parts vermiculite, and 1 part lime. You must sterilize homemade mixes to remove disease-causing organisms. You can buy sterilizing equipment from greenhouse suppliers, but most good-sized soil sterilizers are quite expensive. Some gardeners sterilize small batches of soil in a household oven, baking it at 200°F for an hour. This practice is certainly effective, if odorous.

Bonemeal

Peat

Lime

Perlite

Vermiculite

Washed sand

Bark

Potting soil

Pumice

IN PURSUIT OF ORCHIDS

Although you don't need a greenhouse to grow orchids—many will flower quite nicely on a windowsill or even in the basement under lights (where I once had more than a thousand flourishing away)—for most orchid growers, the Holy Grail of orchid-dom is to someday, somehow have a greenhouse. If you already have a greenhouse and don't yet have orchids, it's likely that a horticultural love affair is in your future, for orchids and greenhouses make perfect companions.

To my mind, the best thing about a greenhouse is the Eden it provides in the midst of winter, when many orchids have their prime flowering time. Surrounded with ever-changing blooms, colors, shapes, and fragrances, you'll be thought a magician of a horticulturist. In truth, growing orchids is not all that difficult.

There are hundreds of thousands of different kinds of orchids—more than 20,000 species alone, and a vast array of hybrids—and the greenhouse's humidity and light allow you to grow them more easily than any other space. But orchids love niches; they are among the most adaptable plants on earth, surviving everywhere from Amazonian rain forests to Arctic snows. The trick is to create the microenvironment that suits each one. If you are just starting out, first decide how much you are willing to invest in climate control. Then pick orchids suitable for your conditions. Unfortunately, if you're like me, the orchid passion has struck, and you fall madly in love with certain plants rather than making calm-headed decisions about suitability.

Orchids are generally classified by their preference in temperatures, and most orchid catalogs indicate what type each orchid is: Warm-growing orchids prefer night temperatures no lower than 60°F. These include such classics as Phalaenopsis, Vanda, and mottled-leaved Paphiopedilum. Intermediate-growing orchids want the minimum night temperature to drop to 55°F. Many Cattleya types and most Oncidium fall into this range. Cool-growing orchids flourish when minimum night temperatures drop as low as 45°F. The most common type is Cymbidium. A number of orchids, such as many Dendrobium, go into a cool dormancy period, often shedding leaves, for parts of the year, but are intermediate or even warm growers the rest of the time.

In addition to having a minimum temperature, some orchids also have a maximum day temperature requirement, giving them a narrow range; these more finicky types may require cooling in hot weather as well as heating in cold weather. Notable among them are Masdevallia and Odontoglossum. A maximum-minimum thermometer will identify the warm and cool spots in the greenhouse.

One trick for growing warmth-loving orchids without having to overwarm them is to provide bottom heat. Phalaenopsis, for instance, grow well with electric propagation mats under their pots when the air temperature drops below the level they prefer. An excellent way to keep temperatures moderate is to dig the greenhouse foundation a foot or two below ground and essentially sink the structure into the earth, which will insulate

Author and photographer judywhite is a past trustee of the American Orchid Society and winner of its highest journalism award as well as the prestigious Silver Medal for building its web site, www.orchidweb.org. She has grown orchids in every conceivable place she could think of, and a lot of inconceivable ones to boot. judy lives in New Jersey and Oundle, England.

it. Choose double glazing or twin-wall polycarbonate. Keep everything well caulked and well ventilated, even in the tiniest greenhouse.

All orchids love humidity above 50 percent, so one of the best heat sources for an orchid greenhouse is a water-heated radiator, circulating either hot water or steam. Ducted hot-air systems and electric heat can be very drying. Orchids are sensitive to the ethylene given off by propane heaters, so it's best to avoid these; if you need to use bottled gas, place the tank outside the greenhouse. Install a backup emergency heating system with an alarm sensor triggered by dropping temperatures. I know of far too many cases in which a heating failure decimated a magnificent and expensive collection overnight.

Automatic side and roof vents (in conjunction with fans), humidity systems, and fertilizer dispensers are all wonderful inventions. Movable sliding benches with mesh bottoms and lots of tiers are also high on my wish list, as are a hose mounted on a sliding pulley system and a gravel floor that drains well.

I stay away from overhead watering systems, however, because they can promote orchid rot and spread fungal and bacterial diseases. I like to water my orchids by hand every day, which also lets me take stock and spot any problems. If this is too time-consuming for your schedule, invest in an automatic drip-watering system with individual emitters within each orchid pot.

As most orchids grow on the sides of trees in nature, they do best in pots with bark chips and lots of drainage holes. Use the thickness of the roots as a guide for potting mix: coarse fir bark for the thickest, medium fir bark for most types, and fine seedlings grade bark for tiny roots. Rather than relying on pesticides, I release beneficial insects to prey on orchid pests. The lacewing is the best all-around predator, devouring aphids, mites, and whiteflies.

When it comes to building an orchid greenhouse, though, the best advice of all is this: Build the biggest one you can, right from the start. Even then, you'll be out of room so fast you won't believe your eyes, for orchids are a passion you'll never outgrow.

judywhite

Encyclia tampensis

You've got your trays of vigorous seedlings stacked up on greenhouse shelves. Soon they'll be ready for potting up and transplanting outdoors.

FROM TINY SEEDS

Simply put, a seed is an embryonic plant enclosed in a protective coat. The seed contains enough food to last until the seedling's first true leaves (the second pair of leaves to unfurl) start to make the sugars that nourish the plant. As the sprouting leaves emerge, a radical, or initial root, travels downward to anchor the plant.

Plan your spring sowing so you'll have seedlings ready to plant out soon after the last frost date. Get this date from a local source, such as the Cooperative Extension Office or a reliable local nursery. The seed packet usually indicates the time seedlings take to reach the transplanting stage—use this number to count back from the frost date. Late sowing may not be a problem in areas with long growing seasons, but in short-summer regions a delay can mean your plants never fully mature

in the garden. For sowing cool-season plants in warmer areas, calculate backward from the time that temperatures will remain consistently cool outdoors.

Timing is less important for plants that will stay in the greenhouse. But because light values do affect plants, cool-season crops seem to grow best in the greenhouse from fall through spring, and warm-season crops thrive during spring and summer months.

SEEDLING GROWTH

Your success rate with germination depends a great deal on how you handle your seeds. Seeds need a careful balance of air, water, and warmth. Some species, like begonias, also require light. Traditional advice was to sow seeds thickly in a large flat and "prick out" or thin seedlings once they developed their second or third set of true leaves. However, seedlings grown this way can become tall, spindly, and weak as they compete with each other to reach more light. Sowing in individual cell packs results in stockier, healthier seedlings.

Most packaged seeds are ready to plant, but seed you've harvested yourself may require special treatment. Some plants native to cold regions require a chilling period, or stratification, to retard germination. Other seeds must be nicked (scarified) to simulate passage through a bird's digestive system. To stratify seeds, soak them in water for 24 hours, then place them in a bag filled with a moist peat-and-sand mix. Refrigerate at 34 to 41°F for 4 to 12 weeks. Rubbing seeds with a file or sandpaper will scarify seed coats.

To start, fill your seed containers with a growing mix (page 65) and moisten it lightly with warm water. Next, plant the seeds at the appropriate depth—a germinating seed planted too deep can suffocate before it reaches the surface. As a general rule, cover seeds with mix equal to two to three times the seed's length. For tiny seeds, apply a light sprinkling of vermiculite or fine sand. Press down on the surface gently. To prevent the seeds from washing away and to keep the soil moist, you can also cover them with a thin layer of chicken grit or clay kitty litter, or with peat moss, which contains a natural fungicide.

At this point, keep the seed container moist and warm, between 70 and 80°F. You can cover the containers loosely with plastic wrap or wet newspaper to hold in moisture, but this may also promote the growth of damping-off fungus (page 89). Remove any coverings when seedlings emerge.

Once the first true leaves unfold, remove the seedlings from propagation heat and place them in a cooler area of the greenhouse. Begin fertilizing with either a special seed-starting formula or with a standard fertilizer at half strength.

Seedlings benefit from 12 to 16 hours of light each day. This can be a combination of daylight and artificial lighting (page 40). If your seedlings receive primarily natural light, rotate their containers a quarter turn each day. Gently ruffle seedlings with your hand to help keep them short and stout.

Lastly, remember to label your seed trays with the species, variety, and date. Your most valuable growing tools are detailed records of your previous successes and failures.

MOVING ON

Seedlings are ready for thinning when they produce a second set of true leaves. Just snip the excess seedlings with scissors or use your fingers to pinch them at the soil level until the remaining seedlings are at the spacing recommended on the seed packet (usually a few inches apart).

As the seedlings grow, transplant them into larger containers until they are mature enough to plant in their final destination. Seedlings must be handled gently. Turn the cell packs upside down and shake lightly to dislodge the plants with as much of the root ball intact as possible. Place them in a moist growing mix in their new containers. When seedlings have reached 4 to 6 inches tall, pinch off the top set of leaves to encourage side shoots and a bushier plant.

SEEDLING CARE

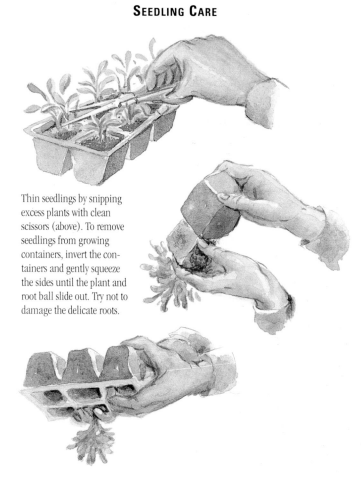

Thin seedlings by snipping excess plants with clean scissors (above). To remove seedlings from growing containers, invert the containers and gently squeeze the sides until the plant and root ball slide out. Try not to damage the delicate roots.

SEEKING OUT SEEDS

Fresh seeds germinate best. When you buy them, make sure they are dated for planting in the current year. Very small seeds may be pelletized, or coated in a pill-like ball, which makes them easier to handle.

Many gardeners harvest seeds from their own plants or from those of friends. Collect seeds when the fruit or seed pods are fully ripe. For vegetables, this is usually past the point at which you would harvest them for eating.

You'll need the right tools to harvest seeds or take cuttings and then transport them safely home. At left is a homemade toolkit for a plant collector. It includes tennis-ball cans for transplants, twine and rubber bands to secure wayward shoots, resealable plastic bags for storing seeds, tools for lifting and cutting plants, labels and a waterproof pen, rooting hormone, a water-filled plastic bottle, and a can of sterile potting mix.

To test the germination potential of seeds, pour them into a glass of water. Those that fall to the bottom are probably viable. You can also place a few seeds between damp paper towels; check for sprouting after a few days.

A CUT ABOVE

Many plants can be propagated from cuttings, given proper warm and moist conditions. To ensure rooting, take cuttings at the right time.

SOFTWOOD AND HERBACEOUS CUTTINGS Take these while the plant is actively growing, from spring through late summer. The growth is fairly soft and flexible, and the cuttings root quickly. You can take softwood cuttings from many species, including forsythia, lavender, magnolia, and weigela. Take herbaceous cuttings from nonwoody plants such as chrysanthemum, coleus, ivy, and pelargonium.

SEMIHARDWOOD CUTTINGS Take these after the active growing season or just after a flush of growth, usually in late spring, summer, or early fall. Trees and shrubs suitable for semihardwood cuttings include broad-leaved evergreens and partially mature deciduous plants such as boxwood, olive, and rhododendron.

HARDWOOD CUTTINGS You can propagate deciduous and narrow-leafed evergreen trees and shrubs, such as species roses and privet, by hardwood cuttings. Take these when the plants are very mature in late summer or dormant from late fall through early spring, depending on your location. A cold greenhouse or cold frame is the best place to overwinter hardwood cuttings (page 78).

LEAF CUTTINGS Some plants develop roots when you place parts of their leaves in a growing medium. African violet, mother-in-law's tongue *(Sansevieria)*, and Begonia rex are propagated in this manner.

ROOT CUTTINGS Other plants have roots that easily develop sprouts and new individuals. Take root cuttings when the plant is dormant, usually in late fall to early spring. Plants suitable for root cutting include Japanese anemone, most cane berries, and Oriental poppy, which has a summer dormancy period instead of a winter one.

Using a single flat, you can create dozens of seedling versions of your favorite plants. Label each cutting carefully, including the date.

ROOTING IN WATER

Placing a shoot in water is a simple way to root basil and some common indoor plants, such as Christmas cactus, coleus, brugmansia, dieffenbachia, English ivy, fuchsia, impatiens, peperomia, philodendron, Pilea spp., spider plant, and wandering Jew. Cut a 3-inch shoot from a full-grown parent plant. Remove all but the top two to four leaves. Secure a piece of hardware cloth over the mouth of a clean glass jar, fill it with water, and stick the cuttings through the holes. Replace the water if it discolors. Remove and pot up the cuttings when the roots are still small enough to fit through the wire holes.

OFFSETS

Some plants, such as hen and chicks, many other succulents, strawberry begonia, and spider plant, produce small plantlets, or offsets, on the end of stems or runners. Others, such as kalanchoe, produce them at leaf margins. These miniatures need only come in contact with moist potting soil to form a root mass. The easiest method is to pot up the offset when it's still attached to the parent plant, keeping it moist until the roots have formed, at which point you can detach it from the parent. Keep the new plantlets out of direct sunlight until they've established themselves.

AIR LAYERING

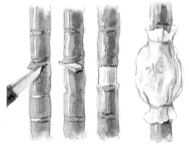

Use air layering to propagate large indoor plants and trees, as well as trees with high branches, such as codiaeum, dracaena, and ficus. Choose an actively growing branch on a parent plant, either early in spring on last year's growth or after a flush of growth in late summer. Begin below a node. Make a slanting cut or remove a ring of bark. Dust the cut with powdered rooting hormone, encase it in damp sphagnum moss, and cover it with plastic wrap to keep it moist. Roots will appear in the sphagnum moss in a few months.

ROOTING SOFTWOOD AND SEMIHARDWOOD CUTTINGS

Sharpen your knife or pruners and disinfect the blades with rubbing alcohol. Dull blades crush the end of your cutting and dirty tools can spread diseases and viruses. Take all cuttings in early morning. Mist the cuttings, and place them in a plastic bag to keep them moist.

1 Fill clean pots or flats with a moist rooting mix. A half-and-half combination of perlite and peat moss works well, as do combinations of these with coarse sand and vermiculite.

2 Choose a healthy parent plant. Cut a stem 8 to 12 inches long. Remove flower buds, flowers, and side shoots. Cut the stem into 3-to-4-inch pieces, each with two or more growing points, or nodes. Cut just below a node—this is where roots will form. Remove all but two to four of the top leaves. Cut large leaves in half to lower the amount of leaf surface from which water can evaporate.

3 Some plants, especially semihardwood cuttings, root more quickly if you dip them in a rooting hormone. Make holes in the rooting mix about twice the diameter of the cutting and 2 inches apart, gently insert the cuttings, and firm them in place. Make sure the cuttings are right side up, although grape and raspberry cuttings root more successfully turned upside down. Lightly mist the cuttings with water and label them with the plant name and date.

Keep the container in a shaded, warm, moist area of the greenhouse. Ventilate covered containers for a few minutes each day.

4 The cuttings will form new leaves once they have rooted in the mix (this may take from one to six months, depending on the plant). To test whether they have rooted sufficiently, tug on the cuttings gently, feeling for resistance. At this point, open the plastic bags to expose the cuttings to drier air, or mist them less frequently.

Transplant the cuttings to individual pots once they have acclimatized to open air. Use deep pots that will hold the developing root systems of trees, shrubs, and perennials. The cuttings should be ready to transplant into the garden during the next planting season.

Some plants, especially houseplants and succulents, respond to different methods of vegetative propagation, such as leaf cuttings.

ROOT CUTTINGS

Almost any plant that produces sprouts from its roots will grow from root cuttings. This includes diverse examples such as bear's breech, blackberry, flowering quince, globe thistle, horse-radish, Japanese anemone, lilac, Oriental poppy, peonies, raspberry, species roses, trumpet vine, and wisteria. Those with thinner, woodier roots are generally easier to propagate.

∼ In the spring, dig up the parent plant and cut finger-thick sections from the roots (below top). Those near the crown will develop shoots most quickly. Slice into 2- to 4-inch sections (below bottom). Do not apply rooting hormone.

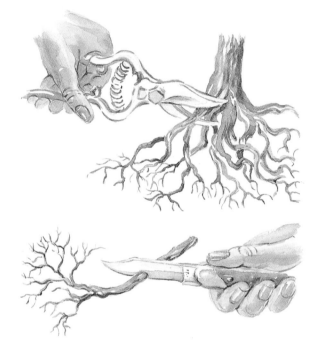

LEAF CUTTINGS

There are three general methods of taking leaf cuttings. All require a propagation container filled with a sterile sand-and-peat mix, or one that combines perlite, peat, and sand or vermiculite. Moisten the mix before placing the cuttings in it. Keep the cuttings out of direct sunlight in a humid environment, either in a propagation box or enclosed in a plastic bag with the temperature between 61 and 64°F.

Root whole leaves (top). This works well with fleshy-leafed plants, such as many succulents, African violets, peperomias, and streptocarpus. Remove leaves with a 1- to 2-inch petiole (the leaf stem) from healthy parent plants. Insert them into the mix.

Place leaves flat on growing mix (below). This method suits rex begonias and other fleshy-leafed species. Make cross-section cuts in the large veins on the bottom surface of mature, healthy leaves. Place the leaf, bottom side down, on the mix. Weight the leaf with pegs or staples so the cuts come into contact with the mix.

Root leaf pieces. Good candidates for this method include many cacti, including epiphytic species. Cut leaf blades into several 3- to 4-inch pieces, making sure to mark the bottom end. Stick three-quarters of the cutting's length into the mix. A new plant will form at the base of each leaf section as the older leaf dies.

∼ If you are rooting only a few cuttings, plant them upright in a container filled with a moistened rooting mix consisting of equal parts peat and either perlite or coarse sand. Root tops should be level with the soil.

Use a mix-filled flat for a larger number of cuttings, laying them horizontally on the media and covering with a ½-inch layer of mix. Water the container well.

∼ Cover the container with plastic or a glass pane and place it in a shaded area of the greenhouse or in a cold frame. When shoots form, move the container into full light. Transplant them into separate pots when shoots are 3 or more inches tall and new roots have formed.

PROPAGATING BULBS

The way in which you propagate bulbs depends on the bulb's underground storage organs. Some bulbs, such as onions and tulips, have tightly packed scales or modified leaves surrounded by a papery covering. Scaly bulbs, such as lilies, have loose, easily separated scales and lack the papery covering.

To scale the former, remove the papery covering, then cut off the bulb's tip and any dead roots with a sharp, clean knife. Stand the bulb vertically and cut it into eight or more equal segments. From each segment, cut pairs of scales with a portion of the basal plate, the compressed stem at the bulb's base. Place these in a bag with moistened vermiculite, and keep in a dark, 68°F location. Bulblets should form in three months; you can then plant them in pots or trays. Place these in a cold frame, and pot them up in the spring or fall.

For scaly bulbs, snap off the scales from the parent bulb and mix them with moistened vermiculite. Place them in a clear, sealed plastic bag that contains as much air as possible. Keep the bag at about 68°F in total darkness. Bulblets will form in about 10 to 12 weeks. Pot the scales and bulblets in a container filled with moistened growing mix, and keep them in a cold frame or cool greenhouse during the spring and summer. Plant them in the garden or in larger pots in the fall when the bulb clusters grow large enough so you can separate them.

Corms, such as *Brodiaea,* colchicum, crocosmia, crocus, freesia, gladiolus, *Sparaxis,* and watsonia, produce miniature cormels at the basal plate, much as scaly bulbs do. Dividing these is a simple process of removing the cormels and planting each in its own container.

Other plants often called bulbs are actually tubers or tuberous roots—really just swollen stems and roots. These include anemone, alstroemeria, arum, caladium, clivia, cyclamen, dahlias, daylilies, and irises. Propagate these in spring by cutting a healthy tuber into sections, each containing an eye, or growing point, and roots. Pot the sections separately and protect them from extreme heat and cold. Once small tubers form, remove them from the parent plant and pot them up. For bearded iris, divide the rhizomes by breaking sections at the natural "waists" between them.

FORCING BULBS

A greenhouse or sunroom is the ideal spot to force bulbs—inducing bloom before the normal flowering season. To make sure the bulbs bloom when you want, you'll need to know whether they require cold treatment. Hardy bulbs, which include amaryllis, hyacinth, crocus, fritillaries, muscari, and tulip, typically bloom after two or three months of cold treatment; you can often buy such bulbs prechilled. Otherwise, place the bulbs in paper bags or containers and keep at 35 to 50°F for the required amount of time. Refrigerators and cold frames are possible cooling sites. When shoots are about 1 inch high, move them to a cool, well-lit spot. As the buds begin to show color, shift them to a warmer, sunny location (65 to 75°F).

Other bulbs, such as anemone, fall-blooming crocus, freesia, narcissus, ranunculus, and scilla, require no chilling and can be potted directly into their containers. Keep them in a cool spot (55 to 60°F) for a few weeks and move them to a warmer spot when the shoots begin to show color.

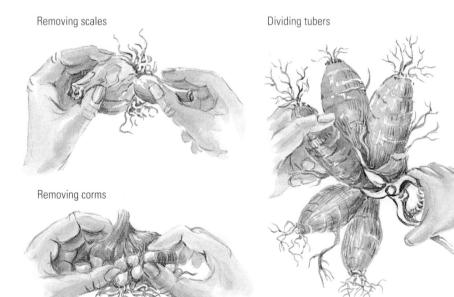

Removing scales

Dividing tubers

Removing corms

MY BROMELIADS

My wife, Sauny, and I were first prompted to collect bromeliads way back in 1970. We were visiting a nursery near Cambria, California. As we were leaving, a staff member said, "Don't fail to see that plant over there." All she could tell us about this strange plant was that it was a member of the family Bromeliaceae, but it had such a peculiar beauty that we were immediately fascinated.

Right away, we went to a specialty nursery in Los Angeles and bought 10 tillandsias. The staff assured us that with proper misting, tillandsias could be grown indoors. Following this advice I promptly killed nine of the ten plants. I took the last one, nailed it to an outdoor porch post, and sprayed it occasionally with the hose. I believe there are descendants of that plant in my greenhouse now.

I now know more about this odd and distinctive group of plants. There are two basic types: the terrestrials, which grow in soil, and the epiphytes, which grow on supporting objects such as trees, fences, and telephone wires. They are not parasitic, however, and so take no nutrients from their support. Many of the terrestrials can be grown as epiphytes, but they require more attention. The epiphytes rarely survive planting in soil; they usually succumb to damp rot.

All bromeliads but one originate in the Western Hemisphere, from Florida and Texas south to Chile and Argentina. West Africa is the origin of the exception, *Pitcairnia feliciana.* There are at present approximately 50 recognized genera and several thousand species of bromeliad. I have a personal prejudice for species plants rather than hybrids because I find the latter are often unreliably labeled.

As a group, bromeliads are relatively pest free, disease free and easy to grow. But because they are of tropical or subtropical origin, they do have certain minimum requirements. While many can survive freezing temperatures (and there are reports of some surviving through snow), it is best to keep them at a minimum of about 40°F. In most parts of the United States, this means you'll need a heated greenhouse. One of the curious habits of bromeliads is their disregard for the seasons. In my greenhouse they seem to bloom only when they are good and ready.

Some bromeliads have special requirements based on their unusual structure. "Tank" or "vase" types have straplike leaves that form a whorl tight enough to hold water. (A frog in South America uses one of these types, a *Neoregelia,* as an incubator for its eggs and relies upon it for survival.) Although the "vase" itself should be continually filled with water, the soil in which the plant grows must be quite dry.

In fact, the chief reason for bromeliad failure is inappropriate watering. The roots of bromeliads, even the terrestrials, are an anchoring mechanism and do not provide the plant with much nourishment. Overwatering leads to damp rot. Ephiphytic types are liable to trap water inside, which can kill them overnight. The key is to hang these types upside down so they drain properly.

Charles Dills is a former professor of chemistry and an avid grower of bromeliads. He lives in San Luis Obispo, California, where he and his wife, Sauny, are actively involved with the creation of a new botanical garden. Charles maintains a web site devoted to his favorite plants at www.charlies-web.com. You can find further sources of information about bromeliads on page 110.

Many bromeliads are quite unfriendly, with irritating spines that can become embedded in your skin. Some of the spines, usually from plants in the genus *Puya* or *Bromelia,* can be so fierce that the plants are used in South America as a barrier. *Puya berteroniana,* for instance, forms a dense 4-foot-high clump of straplike, pointed, spiny leaves with an inflorescence of blue petals up to 11 feet tall, more than enough to keep wild animals—or burglars—at bay!

Many growers concoct special mixes for their terrestrials, but I have found that regular potting mixes work just fine. I add some drainage material from time to time—sand, scoria, rice hulls, or white rocks. I have no proof that this helps, but it makes me feel better. Likewise, I feed my plants every few months with half-strength fertilizer applied as a foliar feed, then I rinse off any residue a few days later.

Sometimes aphids and scale are a problem; they can be treated with the appropriate pesticide (as a chemist, of course, I am always sure to read the label), or daubed with an alcohol-soaked cotton swab, or sprayed with soapy water.

Here in San Luis Obispo the temperature usually varies between an occasional and brief low in the 30s to a rare high of about 85°F. We house our bromeliads in a homemade redwood-and-glass greenhouse. I built the greenhouse with a frame of 4-by-4-inch posts anchored in concrete. The windows are 3 by 4 feet, each with nine small panes set into their mullions and held in place by metal point framers. The three-sided roof rises 13 feet and is covered with 15 tempered-glass shower doors. The structure faces south but is shaded in the afternoon by some trees.

Inside is an exhaust fan that is automatically activated when the temperature reaches 85°F. If it gets much hotter than this, I swivel one of the windows open. To maintain the interior at a minimum of 45°F, I plan to buy a heater.

Sauny designed a "Rube Goldberg" watering system that might surprise an expert, but it seems to work. It consists of ¾-inch PVC pipe to which we have attached whirligig lawn sprinklers. We like to think it imitates a jungle shower.

If I could make changes to the greenhouse, I'd first make it bigger. Then I would add automatic humidity and temperature controls. My ideal is the Princess of Wales Conservatory at Kew Gardens, London, which has 11 different areas, all controlled by computers.

I recommend that you buy bromeliads from a reputable dealer rather than a general nursery; it's the only way to know what you are getting. I recently saw a basket of tillandsias in a pet store that were half-dead and mostly mislabeled. One reason for this is that bromeliads are usually referred to by their Latin names rather than common names, with the major exceptions of pineapple and Spanish moss. Common names, after all, can be treacherous. The same name can be used for several different plants that are not even in the same family!

You're probably still wondering about the plant that originally piqued my interest. Last July, we gave a plant to the fledgling San Luis Obispo Botanical Garden. When I saw it bloom for the first time, I exclaimed, "I think that's it!" Just like the plant in the Cambria nursery, this is the Chilean native *Puya alpestris,* which has a striking inflorescence more than 3 feet long. I enjoy watching visitors to the garden who, fascinated by this strange plant, feel compelled to touch its flaring blue petals to see if they are real.

Charles E. Sill

It's child's play to plant out seedlings, but prepare garden soil thoroughly before putting them in the ground.

THE GREAT OUTDOORS

To your cosseted plants, the garden is a whole new world of wind, temperature, and predators. To help them survive, you'll need to harden them off, or slowly accustom them to the outside climate, starting about ten days before you transplant them outside for good.

Knowing when to transplant is critical. A week of warm weather in early spring may tempt you to put seedlings outside, but the season's last frost or an early heat wave might destroy your hard work. This is a good reason to stagger your plantings; you can set out a second batch if you lose the first one to bad weather. It's a good idea to call your Cooperative Extension agent or a local agricultural association around the time you're hoping to transplant and ask about any approaching unseasonable weather.

You can harden off seedlings when they develop two to three sets of true leaves. On their first trip outside, keep them in a shady area protected from the wind, leaving them outside for only a few hours. During the next eight to nine days, gradually increase sun exposure and the amount of time they spend outside. If possible, keep the plants outside all night the evening before you transplant them into the garden. Choose a cloudy, drizzly day for planting out, or plant in the late afternoon to protect plants from the sun's drying effects. Make sure you water both plants and garden soil before and after transplanting, and maintain consistent soil moisture until the plants are well established.

PLANTING TECHNIQUES

Greenhouse-raised plants headed for your garden have the best chance of survival if you plant them with special care. Prepare the garden bed by loosening the soil to a depth of 8 to 12 inches and amending it with compost and a handful of slow-release fertilizer. Dig a fairly large hole—12-inch-square for a plant in a 4-inch pot, for instance. Turn the potted plants upside down and carefully lift off the pot. If the roots are compacted or rootbound, make up to four ¼-inch vertical cuts through the root ball with a sharp knife. Otherwise, simply loosen or fluff the roots slightly with your fingers to encourage them to grow outward into the soil. Place the plant in the hole, the crown at the same level as in the pot. Firm the soil around the plant, but not too tightly. Encircling it with a small ridge of soil will hold water around the plant and let it soak deeply into the soil. Cover the soil with a layer of mulch to keep it cool and moist.

PEAT POT PLANTING

Plants grown in peat pots may be set directly into the ground, but they must still be hardened off. To plant, soak the pots in water first, then dig a hole slightly deeper than the pot so you can cover the top completely with soil—if the edges protrude above the surface, they'll draw water away from the roots.

PROTECTING TRANSPLANTS

If you garden in a northern climate, you must contend with a short growing season. To grow vegetable crops to fruition or to get an earlier harvest, some daring gardeners plant their seedlings when the risk of frost still hangs in the air. You can improve your chance of success by growing plants in the greenhouse for as long as possible, or by giving young outdoor transplants some form of protection against the elements. In any climate, the arrival of warm or wet weather in spring can induce a population explosion of slugs, earwigs, and other chewing insects to wreak havoc on unprotected seedlings.

1 Place and secure a bottomless plastic milk jug over tender plants, especially tomatoes, to safeguard them from cold, birds, and wind.

2 Prop up a board or shingle to shade new transplants from the hot sun.

3 Place a cardboard box over transplants to buffer temperatures and protect them from pests. Cut the bottom on three sides to give the box a handy lid.

4 Protect tender plants from late frosts with domed plastic or paper coverings. Lift to ventilate plants during the day.

5 Place a glass cloche, or one made of clear plastic over wire loops, to protect tender plants from frost and insects.

6 Heavy plastic draped over a wooden frame protects seedlings from cold, frosty nights. Ventilate during the day.

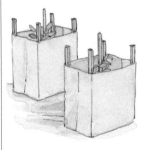

7 Anchor paper bags over new transplants using stakes. Cut a hole in the bag's bottom so it fits over the plant and secure the bottom to deter insects.

8 Place tarpaper or cardboard collars around transplant stems to deter cabbage-root maggots and cutworms.

TRANSPLANTING IN CONTAINERS

You must carefully pot up plants that you intend to grow in containers outdoors or in the greenhouse or conservatory. It's important to choose the right size container. Generally you want to pot up plants in a slightly larger pot, rather than a much bigger one.

Use a good-quality potting mix (it needn't be sterile, as the plants should be beyond the point where they might suffer from damping-off). Fill the new containers with the mix, leaving space to spread out the plants' roots. Water the plants thoroughly. Moist soil from the pot should cling to the roots—the more, the better.

To remove plants from small cell packs, carefully push on the bottom of the individual cells with your thumbs and tip out the plants (page 69). For larger pots, run a knife around the inside edge of the container, then invert the pot and tap it gently to loosen the plant.

When you have removed the plant, gently separate the roots with your fingers. Settle the root ball into the new container and fill in with soil so the top, or crown, of the plant lies about 1 inch below the pot rim. Press in the mix firmly to remove air pockets. Water thoroughly with a fine rose spray.

These hoop-top hot beds provide a cozy spot for germinating seedlings. The covers can be left open during the day to promote air circulation; at night, they should be closed to prevent frost damage.

USING COLD FRAMES

Whether or not you have a greenhouse, a cold frame is a handy addition to the garden. In cool climates, it can help you get a jump on the growing season by providing a warm place to raise seedlings. You can use it to harden off young plants grown in the greenhouse, to store or chill bulbs in winter, and even to grow salad ingredients year-round. You can store tender plants in a cold frame in winter or convert it to a hotbed. It's also an ideal place to store hardwood cuttings (facing page).

HOT BEDS

A hot bed is simply a cold frame with some kind of internal heating source. You can use one as a mini-greenhouse for raising cuttings or seedlings. Originally, composting manure provided the heat to warm a cold frame, but heating cables are a better option today. Spread a 2- to 3-inch layer of sand or vermiculite in the bottom of the frame. Lay down the cable, looping it so that it lies 3 inches away from the sides of the frame. Add another inch of sand, then a sheet of window screen or hardware cloth to protect the cable. Plug the cables into a weatherproof GFCI-protected outlet.

Cold frame construction is very simple. You can make the frame from rot-resistant lumber, masonry blocks, poured concrete, brick, aluminum, or even PVC pipe. Built-in insulation—in the form of solid panels—keeps the frame warmer in very cold-winter climates. Many homemade cold frames have recycled windows as covers; you can also simply buy new window sashes. The glazing needn't be glass, however. You can use almost any material suitable for a greenhouse, including acrylic, polycarbonate, plastic film, or fiberglass (page 31). The lid should slope at an angle and there should be at least 6 inches' difference in height from back to front. You should be able to prop the lid open for ventilation to access the frame's interior. Don't make your cold frame any deeper (from front to back) than 3 feet; it's hard to reach much farther. Make it as long as you like, but each glazing panel must be a practical width and weight, to open and close the cover easily.

The best place to position a cold frame is with the glass sloping toward the south or southwest. Keep a minimum-maximum thermometer inside the frame so you can gauge temperature fluctuations. Open the cover when the temperature reaches about 75°F inside the cold frame. Close it in late afternoon to trap heat for the evening. You can also install a nonelectric automatic vent controller (page 32). On very cold nights, drape the frame with an old blanket or piece of carpet to provide extra insulation. In midsummer, you can cover the glazing with shade paint or cloth.

ROOTING HARDWOOD CUTTINGS

Hardwood cuttings taken when a plant is dormant during fall and winter develop a callus, or an irregular mass of cells, that will eventually form roots. In general, hardwood cuttings need cool temperatures and darkness to remain dormant and form roots. A well-lit, warm greenhouse is not appropriate; to give cuttings the right conditions you should bury them in vermiculite or sand in a cold greenhouse or cold frame. You can significantly improve the cuttings' chance of rooting if you keep their tops cool while also supplying bottom heat to the root zone. In a cool greenhouse you can accomplish this by placing propagation heat mats underneath the box of cuttings.

1 Choose a healthy, mature parent plant. Take pencil-thin, 1- to 2-foot-long cuttings from the previous season's growth, which is usually lighter in color than the old wood.

   Snip off the top 1 or 2 inches of the stem. Cut the remaining stem into 6- to 9-inch pieces, each with two or three nodes. Cut each length about ½ inch above or below a node. Keep track of which end is the top. Dip the bottom of the cutting into rooting hormone.

2 In climates where the ground freezes in winter, bundle the cuttings with the tops facing the same direction and place them in a cold frame or in a box or crate in a cool greenhouse. Cover them with vermiculite or sand.

   In warmer climates, bury the cuttings in an outdoor trench, covering them with soil.

3 Once the hardwood cuttings have rooted, pot them as you would semihardwood cuttings (page 71) for eventual transplanting into the garden. Alternatively, plant the cuttings about 6 inches apart in a protected outdoor area in early spring. Dig a shallow, narrow trench and fill it with an inch or two of sand. Place the cuttings into the sand with the callus end down and just one bud above soil level. Fill the trench with a mixture of soil, perlite, sand, and compost. Firm in and water the cuttings.

4 Keep the cuttings shaded and moist during the growing season. You can plant them permanently in the garden by next fall or spring.

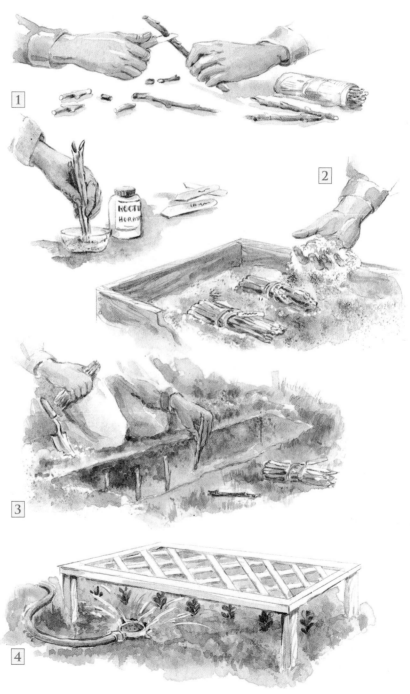

GREENHOUSE BEDS

Growing plants in the greenhouse allows you to monitor and relocate them according to their needs. For some plants, containers can limit root growth and uptake of water and nutrients. If you want bountiful vegetable crops, climbing vines, and fruit and ornamental trees, try one of the following alternatives.

There's virtually no outdoor plant you can't bring into the greenhouse. In-ground beds provide plenty of room for roots to spread, resulting in correspondingly lush top growth.

TYPES OF BEDS

You have a choice of beds in the greenhouse—above ground or below ground. If your greenhouse does not have a concrete subfloor, you can dig beds directly into the ground. In-ground beds allow more vertical growing space for climbing and trellised crops. However, they also require more bending and digging.

Prepare and treat indoor beds as you would an outdoor garden plot by turning the soil and amending it with organic matter. If your soil has poor drainage, add a bottom layer of gravel when you prepare the beds. A few weeks before planting in your beds, apply one bucket of manure, leaf mold, or compost for every square yard of bed. If your greenhouse beds are full year-round, you can maintain good soil fertility by regular mulching and rotating crops.

If your soil is poor, or if you want to garden year-round in a cold region, you can install raised beds in the greenhouse. Raised beds usually receive more light and they are easier to work in, especially in a limited greenhouse space. Surround the bed with an outer frame built of rot-resistant wood, brick, or concrete. Fill the frame with soil, leaving a few inches empty at the top. If you build beds on top of a concrete slab, you must ensure that the beds are well-drained, either by placing weep holes to the exterior or by breaking through the concrete and installing drains.

GROW BAGS

Plastic grow bags, typically white or opaque, hold roughly 1 to 3 cubic feet of peat, perlite, vermiculite, or a blend of the three. You can use them to grow high-yield vegetable crops, such as tomatoes and greenhouse cucumbers, or salad crops. The inert medium supports the root system, and its sterile nature helps plants get off to a disease-free start. Bag dimensions vary depending on the manufacturer, but some can hold up to three tomato plants each. Because the plant's root system grows throughout the medium, you can use the bags for only one crop cycle. Put the root mass and mix into the compost when the plant has stopped growing.

Lay the grow bags directly on the greenhouse floor or on a slotted potting bench. For proper drainage, cut small slits into the bags about 1 inch from the bottom. Water the bags thoroughly, preferably with warm water, which the growing medium absorbs more readily. A shallow pool of water and nutrients will form in the bottom of the bag. Sow seeds in place, or transplant seedlings into grow bags just as you would in a garden plot (there's no need to harden them off, of course). The greatest challenge with grow bags is to ensure that the soil is constantly moist but not overwatered.

Plant your growing beds as you would outdoor beds. Because greenhouse plants grow fast and dry out quickly, you'll need to watch water and nutrient requirements carefully. Unless you're exceptionally diligent, it's best to keep your beds irrigated with an automatic watering system (page 42).

THE EDIBLE GREENHOUSE

You can grow many types of vegetables and fruits in a well-maintained greenhouse, from common squash to exotic figs. What you harvest depends on your space, equipment, and imagination.

Probably the most important factor is your greenhouse's temperature. Just as they would outdoors, cool-season crops grow best in cool greenhouses (night temperatures below 45°F), and warm-season crops thrive in warm greenhouses (night temperatures above 45°F). Many greenhouses have a tropical or subtropical climate—moist and warm, with high nighttime temperatures. This makes it possible to grow plants such as banana, citrus, or even guava and kiwi.

If you want to grow dwarf fruit trees, it's best to plant them in containers so their roots are confined. Restricting trees to containers also restrains their growth, much as bonsai are kept small.

For more intensive crop production, consider installing one of several types of hydroponic systems. These have many advantages for growing food crops, including keeping the food free of soil and producing a high yield in a limited area (page 82).

SUPPORTING CROPS

Spreading and vining crops will need support as they grow. You can use cages or stakes for tomatoes as you would in the garden. Beans, cucumbers, and squash can vine along poles, netting, or trellises. For high-yield crops, such as tomatoes, cucumber, squash, and grapes, form a support grid by securing string or wire to the structure's glazing bars. Attach nylon netting to a wall to support ornamental climbing vines. With any sort of support, make sure the plant can "breathe" and has plenty of air flow through its leaves to prevent disease.

GREENHOUSE CROPS

WARM GREENHOUSE

TOMATO FAMILY: **eggplant, peppers, tomatoes, tomatillos**

CURCUBITS: **melons, squash, greenhouse cucumbers**

Beans

HERBS: **many kinds**

FRUITS: **avocado, banana, citrus, grapes, fig, kiwi**

COOL GREENHOUSE

COLE CROPS: **broccoli, cabbage, chicory, collards, cress, kale, kohlrabi, radish**

LEAFY GREENS: **endive, lettuce, spinach, Swiss chard**

Peas

Beets

Carrots and parsley

ONION FAMILY: **chives, garlic, leeks, onion**

PLANNING YOUR CROPS

Crops such as grapes, cucumbers, and squash like to spread, so give them plenty of room. Keep in mind that crops like tomato and eggplant need lots of light to ripen their fruits. Overcrowding will limit light, as will shortened winter days. Make sure each plant has plenty of space, and supply supplementary light as needed.

If your space is limited, try growing smaller or dwarf vegetables that take less room and allow you to use your space more efficiently. Some miniature varieties like 'Tom Thumb' lettuce and 'New Hampshire Midget' watermelon are available from mail-order companies. Also try growing just one or two plants of any one crop. Harvest what you need and let them produce a second flush of growth.

Some crops may be difficult or impossible to grow because of their natural requirements. Many fruits and vegetables, including rhubarb, asparagus, and apple, need cold winter temperatures to produce a crop the following year. Ingenious gardeners may find nature's loophole by transferring these crops outside for a cold treatment, but the crop yields may not be worth all the hard work.

Unless you have bees or other pollinating insects in your greenhouse, you will need to pollinate your crops by hand to ensure they yield fruit. For most crops, all it takes is transferring pollen from one flower to another. Do this by either brushing each flower with a fine paintbrush or tapping the blossom to distribute pollen. Tropical fruits can be more difficult to pollinate because they require specific pollinators; when purchasing tropical fruits, make sure to ask about pollination requirements. (Some tropical varieties do not require pollination.) Other plants, such as the European forcing cucumber, are specially bred for greenhouses and need no pollination.

Sooner or later your crop plants will give out and stop producing. Periodically propagate additional plants by seeds or cuttings to replace your current crop. This way you can almost guarantee that you'll be harvesting vegetables and fruits year-round.

Among the advantages of hydroponic growing is a reduction in the number of pests and diseases common to soil-grown plants.

HYDROPONICS

Hydroponics may conjure up images of space-age technology, but it actually works on the simple concept of surrounding plant roots with water and nutrients rather than soil. Although the technique gained popularity in the 1970s, modern hydroponic cultivation has been around since the early part of the century. Commercial greenhouses use hydroponics because they require less labor than traditional growing methods.

MEDIA- AND WATER-BASED SYSTEMS

A greenhouse hydroponic system may be either media based or solely water based. Media-based systems use a substrate—pea gravel, sand, expanded shale, perlite, vermiculite, rock wool, sawdust, wood chips, or other soilless material—to support the growing plant. The media surround the roots with a nutrient solution, keeping them moist between waterings. Although media-based systems are reliable and simple to use, the media itself can be messy and costly.

A water-based system supplies plant roots with a constant flow of nutrient solution. Rock wool cubes or collars lend plants support in lieu of growing media. These systems are lighter and more compact than media-based systems.

HYDROPONIC PHILOSOPHY

Growers who like hydroponics tend to become quite passionate about the system. It's true that hydroponic systems save time and extra work because they are easily automated with timers and self-watering systems. Because you don't use media, weeds and soil-borne diseases are reduced. These systems also save space, allowing gardeners to maximize growing areas in the greenhouse.

Hydroponics can have its drawbacks, however. Getting a system up and running—and keeping it running—calls for continued investment in media, nutrient solution, and equipment. You lose the advantages of soil-borne beneficial organisms.

When setting up a hydroponic system for the first time, keep it simple. Consider your current space, lighting, and financial limitations before choosing a system. Also consider how much time you have to devote to regular maintenance.

SAND AND GRAVEL SYSTEMS

Sand and pea-gravel systems are some of the oldest and easiest hydroponic techniques. Leak-proof growing beds are filled with sand or gravel, and plants grow directly in the media. Media-based systems require irrigation cycles two to three times each day, depending on sand and gravel particle size. The smaller the particle size, the more tightly the media holds water.

Sand and gravel have the advantage of being fairly inexpensive and easy to obtain. They're also simple to clean and have a long life. If using sand, be sure to use coarse-textured sand. Fine sand tends to hold too much water, depriving roots of oxygen.

These media do become heavy and cumbersome when wet, so make sure you have a stable bench structure that can handle the weight. Algal growth may also pose a problem on the sand surface if kept too wet.

EBB-AND-FLOOD SYSTEMS

The concept behind ebb-and-flood hydroponic systems is to periodically flood and drain plants growing in reservoirs. Plants are placed in media-filled pots or rock wool cubes which provide support and moisture once the reservoirs drain.

The ebb-and-flood system in its simplest form consists of a leakproof growing tray connected by a tube to a container holding nutrient solution. When the container is raised, solution flows into the growing tray. Lowering the container once the media is saturated causes the solution to drain from the system. This set-up is easily automated by adding a pump and a timer to the solution container. Automating the system lets you leave it for a day or two without worrying.

NUTRIENT FILM TECHNIQUE (NFT) SYSTEMS

The NFT system is a water-based hydroponic method popular in both hobby and commercial greenhouses. It uses a system of channels or pipes through which a pump continuously circulates nutrient solution. Rock wool cubes or sturdy supports hold plants in the pipes so their root tips are constantly washed with solution. A flowing solution helps increase oxygen supply to the roots and keep plants healthy.

Because it's water-based, an NFT system must be automated to ensure that roots are constantly wetted by nutrient solution. A power outage or mechanical breakdown can potentially injure or kill plants in these systems. The system loses water through the plants' consumption and evaporation, so the nutrient solution requires constant monitoring. NFT does have the advantage of being easy to install and more lightweight and compact than media-based systems, and it also doesn't present the inconvenience of media disposal.

HERE'S A SOLUTION

One of the main benefits of hydroponics is the compact nature of its systems. You can suspend NFT pipes anywhere there is headspace (above) in the greenhouse, even turning them vertically. Or you can build or purchase bench systems such as the one shown below. This one features clay pellets for growing larger plants in mesh pots and rock wool cubes that fit into a plastic propagator for seedlings and cuttings, along with a complete line of nutrient solutions.

GROWING CACTUS AND SUCCULENTS

As a horticulturist, I deal with many different kinds of plants, but it's the atypical ones that interest me the most. My first such plant was a gift from my grandmother on my sixth birthday. It was a *Notocactus leninghousii,* also called a golden torch cactus. I don't remember how long it survived, but I do remember that I was fascinated by it.

The kit greenhouse where I have my collection is made by the Santa Barbara Greenhouse company. It is redwood, 6 feet wide by 8 feet long, with slat benches and slightly textured fiberglass glazing. I built it in a sunny (south-facing) asphalt-covered side yard, and I paved the floor. It's easier to keep clean, and soil-dwelling pests are less of a problem.

I have about 300 succulent plants, 200 of them inside the greenhouse. The others live outside under a clear polycarbonate patio cover or on a light table inside the house. I also have a few decorative low-light types dotted around the house. Although serious collectors have thousands of plants, this is plenty to keep me busy. I probably spend 1 to 1½ hours per week maintaining my collection in the summer, and 15 minutes or so in the winter. The good thing about succulents is that there is always something that *could* be done with them, but not too much that *has* to be done with them.

I'm lucky that I don't have to go to great expense or trouble to heat and cool my greenhouse. Most of my plants can survive at temperatures down to about 30°F. I measure the temperature with a minimum-maximum thermometer and have a floor heater and a fan to guard against extreme winter cold. I rely on custom-made canvas covers that I roll over the roof at night; they prevent some heat loss and raise the temperature inside the greenhouse by several degrees. If I am very concerned about the cold, I bring some of the more expensive or sensitive species (such as *Euphorbia*) indoors.

My area is more likely to be too hot than too cold, so in the summer I open vents and use shade cloth that is 50 percent white to keep direct sun off the plants and to maintain the greenhouse at a temperature 5 to 10°F cooler than outside. Surprisingly, many succulents originate from partly shaded microenvironments—within the shelter of a tree or rock, for instance, or on the north side of a canyon. Sometimes only a few hours of direct sun on a hot day can sunscald a sensitive or unacclimated plant.

Most succulents originate in arid regions and can suffer from "wet foliage" diseases. Growers in the humid southern United States and tropical areas may need to provide ventilation with electric fans, cooling units, and dehumidifiers. In these areas, soils may also dry more slowly due to high humidity and reduced water uptake by the plant. This calls for less frequent watering and soil mixes that drain well. However, not all succulents are from desert environments, and you can select succulent plants that tolerate higher humidity—for example "jungle succulents" such as *Schlumbergera*, the popular Christmas cactus.

Deborah Ellis is a consulting arborist and horticulturist in Saratoga, California. Her work involves a broad range of advisory services for nurseries, planners, growers, insurance companies, and many others. In addition to her interest in spiky indoor plants, she loves to garden outdoors with California native plants.

Correct watering is essential, but watering guidelines for cacti and succulent plants can be confusing. There is no rule of thumb, but most succulents do like to dry out between waterings. After years of growing plants, I can judge the water requirement of my smaller plants by lifting the pots and feeling how heavy they are. Small containers dry out faster than large ones, so during the summer I have to water some of my 2- or 3-inch pots twice a week. Some succulents indicate that they need water by their appearance. For example, I will not water certain plants until they begin to wrinkle visibly.

A bonus of hand-watering succulents in a greenhouse is that you can grow plants from all around the world with different moisture needs. I water plants with a watering can that has a small, ⅜-inch spout. Too much water coming out quickly can injure the shallow, fine roots of small plants, as well as disrupt the gravel topdressing or the bare soil surface. I also have a small-diameter water-wand hose attachment for watering some of the larger plants. I always try to fill my watering can from the rain barrel, which is right outside the greenhouse door.

Cactus growers tend to have their own personal preferences about soil mixes. I make my own soil mix from regular houseplant potting soil, perlite, and sand, and tailor the soil to meet the requirements of individual plants—some prefer less gritty soil. I generally fertilize succulents once a month during an active growth period, with a water-soluble houseplant fertilizer at half strength.

Sanitation is all-important. Once a year I remove everything from the greenhouse and spray inside and out with a high-pressure hose attachment. I also scrub the outside of the roof, which tends to collect dust and debris. Inside the greenhouse, the underside of the benches must be clean—it is a favorite hiding place of mealybugs, which are the succulent grower's number one problem. Because the plants are not rained upon, they also tend to collect dust, where mites thrive. To combat this, I choose a cloudy day at least once a year and spray all the greenhouse plants with water, except the ones with fuzzy or hairy foliage, which the water would stain.

Clay and plastic pots are the most common succulent containers. Which type is better is a heated topic among growers. I find plastic pots better for plants that I don't want to dry out too fast. I place most of my show plants in clay or stoneware pots for aesthetics, but I've also seen some very good show plants in plastic pots.

I get plants from many sources, including other collectors, cactus club meetings and shows, mail-order or retail nurseries that specialize in cacti and succulents (page 111), and regular retail nurseries. Succulents can be expensive, but the secret to a large collection is to purchase smaller, less costly specimens. If you're like me, however, you won't be able to resist an occasional splurge on a rare or atypical plant!

Debbie Ellis

85

TROUBLESHOOTING

On the following pages, you'll find descriptions and controls for the most common cultural problems, diseases, and pests. But vigilant maintenance goes a long way to preventing disease or pest outbreaks in the greenhouse. Keep air moving with fans and vents. Give plants plenty of room to breathe and try not to overwater or underwater. Also, make sure you disinfect pruners and other tools with rubbing alcohol before and after working with any plant material.

New plant arrivals are a prime source of infestations. If possible, isolate new plants until you are sure they contain no unwanted guests. Check your plants for insects and diseases often, looking at both the top and bottom of the leaves and the surface of the soil. If you do find an infested plant, move it immediately to an isolated area. Insects can crawl though windows, doors, vents, and cracks. Screen your vents, and check and repair them frequently, and repair broken and cracked glazing.

Weed seeds can blow through vents, arrive with new plants, or hitch a ride on clothing and pets. Cracks in cement, gravel floors, and propagation beds are perfect places for weed seeds to nestle and grow. Some, such as the common greenhouse weed wood sorrel *(Oxalis stricta),* are beautiful plants, but they can harbor aphids, thrips, and other damaging insects. Removing all weeds from the greenhouse will help you control pest populations and make your space look neat and clean. Spot-spray hard-to-remove weeds with an herbicide such as glyphosate, protecting your nearby potted and bedded plants.

OTHER PROBLEMS

Wild birds may help rid an outdoor garden of insects, but they can cause damage flying about inside a greenhouse, knocking over pots or breaking glass in a frightened attempt to escape. If birds frequently fly into greenhouse glazing, try placing shimmering objects in the windows to frighten them away.

Keep rodents of all kinds out of the greenhouse. They can chew roots and wooden structures, and contaminate sterilized potting mixes. Mice nibble on stored or newly planted seeds. Place screens over ground-level vents and fans. Try capturing rodents with humane cages and mouse traps. Bait will kill rodents, but you must regularly inspect for dead animals—an unpleasant task. A better solution is to encourage the family cat to frequent the greenhouse.

TOP TO BOTTOM: Fluoride injury, iron deficiency, magnesium deficiency, overwatered plant.

CULTURAL PROBLEMS

PROBLEM	CAUSES	SOLUTION
Seeds fail to germinate	Old seeds Seeds planted too deep Seeds washed out of the planting mix	Purchase fresh seeds, and plant at the proper depth in well-aerated, loosened media Water gently
Leggy seedlings bending toward light source	Too little light	Provide more light Rotate containers ¼ turn each day
Wilted cuttings	Low humidity	Mist regularly Cover until rooted
Malformed or puckered leaves	Inconsistent watering	Water plants regularly according to their needs and the weather conditions
Dropping buds and flowers	Dry conditions Sudden temperature changes	Increase humidity Regulate temperatures and change plant locations
Slowly yellowing leaves that drop	Overwatering	Allow soil to dry slightly between waterings
Yellowing, dropping leaves and slowed growth	Temperature too cool	Move plant to warmer section of greenhouse or provide more heat
Yellowing new leaves	Iron deficiency	Provide chelated trace elements and iron
Yellowing older leaves	Low temperatures	Adjust temperatures and move plants from cold areas of the greenhouse
Yellowing older leaves with green veins	Magnesium deficiency	Apply Epsom salts (magnesium sulfate) to soil or as a foliar spray
Pale, yellowing leaves covering plant	Nitrogen deficiency	Apply a high-nitrogen fertilizer
Browning leaf tips and edges	Dry air Alkaline soil or water Potassium deficiency Fluoride damage	Increase humidity Use rainwater or soft water in hard-water areas Apply a well-balanced fertilizer Use rainwater or distilled water
Blossom drop on fruiting plants	Incorrect temperature	Raise or lower temperature
Fruit fails to set, rots, or shrivels	No pollination	Buy self-fruitful varieties Pollinate by hand
Algae and moss growth on pot surface	Overwatering	Remove algae and moss Decrease watering frequency and humidity levels
Pale brown spots on leaves	Sunscald	Provide shade or move plants to a shady location, particularly during peak sun hours Provide sufficient water

KEEP IT CLEAN

Warm weather is an ideal time for greenhousekeeping, as you can remove your plants from the greenhouse and leave them outside overnight.

Start by cleaning and sweeping floors and other surfaces. Scrub benches and framing with a household disinfectant listed for glass, cement, metal, and aluminum. Algae grow readily on wet cement and humid glass, so disinfect these areas as well with a glass or tile cleaner that contains an algicide. Weed seeds, insects, moss, and algae can find refuge in the gravel on floors or in propagation beds, so washing, disinfecting and sifting the gravel in a mesh tray can help eliminate these problems. If your greenhouse has shade cloth or plastic propagation-box coverings, wash those items as recommended by the manufacturer.

One of the best defenses against predators large and small is to keep the greenhouse tightly sealed, but this can cause heat to build up quickly. A good solution is to cut ordinary window screening material and secure it over vents, especially those near ground level.

To encourage beneficial insects, try not to disturb their nesting areas; a few spiderwebs in the corners do far more good than harm. When bringing plants back in from outdoors, clean off any dead flowers, stems, or leaves, and check to see if any pests have made your plants their new homes.

BENEFICIAL INSECTS AND BIOLOGICAL CONTROLS

Not all insects you find in your greenhouse are pests. Many insect species, and even certain fungi, bacteria, and nematodes, are natural enemies of the pests that cause damage to greenhouse plants. These good bugs attack pests either for food or to lay eggs in them, killing the pests in the process.

While beneficial organisms may not eradicate the entire pest population, they can decrease its numbers enough to make the damage tolerable. They also offer a safe, chemical-free method of pest control. For beneficials to be effective, release them around the afflicted plants and in the greenhouse before pest numbers become severe. Many beneficial insects are most effective if applied from midspring to midfall, except for grub-killing nematodes, which must be applied in late summer. Almost all chemical pest controls can kill beneficial insects, so try to target pests specifically.

In addition, encourage a spider population. A spider can eat up to two times its weight each day, making it more than effective in cleaning up aphids, beetles, flies, and many other insects. Several species of lizard, such as the Western blue-belly, are beneficial in the greenhouse as they also eat many insects. Likewise, encourage a resident toad by placing a commercial or homemade "toad house" in a secluded spot under a bench.

Beneficial nematodes   Assassin bug   Spider

TREATING DISEASES

DISEASE	DESCRIPTION	CONTROLS
Botrytis *(Botrytis cinerea* fungus)	Infections start as water-soaked lesions. Spore masses develop, causing the plant to blacken and wither. Affects many fruits, vegetables, and ornamentals, especially grapes, strawberries, geraniums, and zinnias.	Provide good air circulation and adequate spacing between plants. Limit overhead watering. Remove and destroy all infected plants. For chemical control, apply chlorothalonil only to nonedible plants; apply captan to edibles.
Damping off *(Botrytis, Fusarium, Phytopthora, Pythium,* and *Rhizoctonia* fungus)	Affects very young seedlings. Causes sudden seedling collapse and rot, bare patches in the seedling tray, discoloration of stems, and cottony fungal growth.	Use sterilized containers and starting mix. Plant seeds at the recommended depth. Avoid overwatering and high humidity. Thin seedlings. Spray with a mixture of chamomile tea (1 teabag to 4 cups water). Apply a liquid copper sulfate or copper oxychloride if necessary. Some growing mixes contain fungicides that prevent damping off. Read the label carefully to determine if you can use them on edible plants.
Powdery mildew and downy mildew (fungi)	Affects a wide range of ornamental and edible plants. Thrives when days are warm and nights are cool. Poor light and ventilation also encourage mildew outbreaks. Powdery, round white spots on upper leaf surface. New leaves may be deformed and older leaves turn from a yellowish-green to brown.	Provide plants with plenty of light and air circulation, and keep foliage dry. Remove infected leaves and let the pot dry between waterings. Spray with horticultural oil, sulfur, or a mixture of baking soda and water.
Rust (fungus)	Roses, snapdragons, geraniums, and many fruits and vegetables are susceptible to different rust diseases. Masses of powdery spores ranging from white to yellow or reddish-brown develop on the undersides of leaves. The leaf's top surface may show yellow spotting.	Provide good air circulation and avoid watering plants from above. Make sure plants dry before nighfall. Plant rust-resistant varieties. Remove and destroy affected tissues. Contact your Cooperative Extension Office for advice on chemical control.
Tomato blight (fungus)	Usually attacks tomatoes grown outdoors, but can be a problem in cooler greenhouses. Brown or black blotches develop on leaves. Green fruits develop dark spots or streaks that spread over the fruit until it rots.	Plant resistant cultivars. Remove and destroy affected fruits and leaves. Spray a Bordeaux mixture (of hydrated lime and copper) after flowers bloom.
Viruses	Many plants are susceptible to viruses, most notably chrysanthemums and tomatoes. The large number of viruses results in a range of symptoms. Often, infected plants have mottled or yellowing leaves, spots in the form of concentric rings, curled and stunted leaves, and spotted flowers.	Removing and destroying the entire plant is the best strategy. Control insects that may transmit the viruses. Do not use tobacco products around tomato plants. Wash your hands, and disinfect pruners and equipment before handling plants.

Botrytis   Damping off   Powdery mildew   Rust

PEST CONTROL

PEST	DESCRIPTION	CONTROLS
Ants	Ants vary in color from red to black and in size up to 1 inch long. Some are attracted to sweet foods. Their presence in the greenhouse is usually a nuisance, not a major problem. Ants on citrus, succulents, and other plants may indicate the presence of other pests, which ants "farm" for honeydew.	Remove any food or drinks from the area, and lay out sticky traps or make baits of boric acid and apple jelly. Spray with pyrethrins. For chemical control, apply carbaryl, or baits containing avermectin. Severe infestations may call for the services of a professional pest-control expert.
Aphids	Small (up to ⅛-inch long), pear-shaped, soft-bodied insects that can be white, pink, red, green, or black; some are winged. Aphids tend to move slowly and cluster together. They suck plant juices and leave a clear sticky secretion called honeydew. A fungus called sooty mold can grow on honeydew, making leaves appear black. Infected leaves, buds, flowers, and stems curl, yellow, and become stunted.	Use an alcohol-soaked cotton swab to remove individual aphids. Dust infected plants with diatomaceous earth. Encourage beneficial insects such as lacewings, ladybugs, and soldier beetles. Blast aphids off plants with water. Treat plants with insecticidal soap, hot-pepper wax, cinnamon oil–based insecticide, or pyrethrins. For chemical control, apply acephate, or malathion.
Caterpillars	Caterpillars are the larval form of many different species of butterflies, moths, and other insects. They vary in size and color. Caterpillars eat leaves and flower petals, leaving large holes or even defoliating plants.	Remove caterpillars by hand. For large infestations, release the biological control *Bacillus thuringiensis*. Spray with rotenone, neem, or pyrethrins.
Earwigs, sowbugs, snails and slugs	The familiar, ¾-inch-long earwig has pointed pincers on the rear of its abdomen and quickly crawls away when bothered. Sowbugs are grey crustaceans with segmented backs. Both insects nibble seedlings and plant leaves and flowers, but are usually more beneficial than damaging. Snails and slugs chew holes in foliage and flowers, leaving visible "slime" trails.	Clear of plant debris. To trap sowbugs and earwigs, place a rolled newspaper on the floor at night and shake the hidden insects into soapy water the next morning. (Move sowbugs to the compost heap, where they will happily feed on decaying vegetation.) For chemical control of earwigs, spray with or place commercial poison earwig traps. Hand pick slugs and snails at night or use non-toxic snail bait.
Leafhoppers	There are many species of leafhoppers, most slender and wedge-shaped with a triangular head. Color varies from brown to green, and many have brightly colored wings. Leafhoppers jump quickly and fly away when bothered. They suck plant juices from stems and lower leaf surfaces, leaving them coarse and dappled.	Encourage beneficial insects such as pirate bugs, ladybugs, lacewings, spiders, and parasitic wasps. Spray with insecticidal soap. For chemical control, use pyrethrum, rotenone, neem, carbaryl, or malathion.
Leaf miners	These tiny, pale green fly larvae tunnel within leaves, leaving winding, almost transparent trails. For older plants, the damage is mainly cosmetic, except in large infestations, when it can cause chlorophyll depletions and weaken the plants. Seedlings, however, can die outright.	Pick and destroy damaged leaves. Release and encourage beneficial insects such as parasitic wasps. Chemical control is not effective.
Flea beetles	Small (¹⁄₁₀-inch), shiny, oval beetles, normally blue-black, brown, or green. Many have markings on their backs. These beetles jump like fleas and prefer hot, dry weather. They chew small holes in plant leaves.	Prevent infestations by keeping the growing mix well-watered, which discourages flea beetles from laying eggs. Misting leaves with water will dislodge some insects. Apply insecticidal soap. For chemical control, apply carbaryl or rotenone.
Mealybugs	These oval, soft-bodied insects form white cottony masses along stems and leaves. They suck plant juices and weaken plant tissues, especially new growth. This makes leaves stunted, curled, spotted, and yellowed, resulting in leaf drop. Mealybugs exude a sticky honeydew.	A strong stream of water should remove mealybugs, as will an alcohol-dipped cotton swab. Release beneficial insects like the mealybug destroyer (*Cryptolaemus montrouzieri*, or "crypto"), parasitic wasps, and lacewings. Control ants, which "farm" mealybug populations for honeydew. Spray with insecticidal soap, horticultural oil, pyrethrins, or hot-pepper spray.

PEST	DESCRIPTION	CONTROLS
Mites	Spider mites are very small (¼ inch). They are normally red, pale green, or yellow. Tarsonemid mites (the cyclamen and broad mites) are microscopically small. Mites suck plant juices from leaves and spin feathery webs on their undersides. Damaged leaves appear speckled at first, then become bronze or gray, and eventually dry, curl, and drop. Spider mite infestations develop in hot, dry weather.	Increase humidity. Isolate infested plants. Use a heavy spray of water to dislodge small numbers of mites. Release beneficial insects such as ladybugs, lacewings, and predatory mites. Spray plants with insecticidal soap, horticultural oil, or cinnamon oil–based insecticide. Chemical controls are not effective.
Scale insects	Scale insects look like tiny barnacles, clumped together on stems and leaves. They may be yellow, white, or brown. Adults are wingless and immobile. Leaves may turn yellow and drop. Some scales produce honeydew, encouraging sooty mold populations.	Scrape off scales with a fingernail or a dull knife, or dab with an alcohol-soaked swab. Apply horticultural oils and insecticidal soaps (use a half-strength soap for ferns). Release beneficial insects such as lacewings, parasitic wasps, and beetles. Chemical controls are not effective; destroy severely affected plants.
Thrips	Thrips are tiny (less than 1/20 inch long). Through a hand lens they appear brown, yellow, or black with a rice-shaped body. The insects suck plant juices and scrape chlorophyll from leaves and flowers, causing white spots on flower petals. Leaves look silvery and flowers are distorted. Outbreaks peak in hot, dry weather.	Increase humidity and keep plants sufficiently moist. Rinse plants to dislodge insects, and hang yellow sticky cards to trap them. Release beneficial insects such as parasitic wasps, lacewings, and predatory mites and spiders. Spray adults with insecticidal soap, neem, or horticultural oil. Dust leaves with diatomaceous earth or sulfur to kill nymphs.
Weevils	Long-snouted beetle species about 1/3 inch in length, black to brownish-gray, with small, spotted backs. Adults do not fly and larvae are chunky white grubs about ½ inch long. Adult weevils chew leaf margins. Larvae feed on roots and underground stems, stunting growth, causing wilting, and eventually killing the plant.	Clear dead leaves and debris from around plants. Knock weevils off leaves onto a sheet of paper while they feed at night and then drown them. Apply nematodes, a biological control for weevil grubs, to the soil. For adults, spray leaves with acephate, neem, or rotenone.
Whiteflies	Small (⅛-inch), white, mothlike, winged insects. Larvae are flattened, almost colorless ovals resembling scale insects. Both adults and larvae feed in groups and suck plants for juice, secreting a sticky honeydew. Leaves become stippled yellow, then curl and turn brown. When disturbed, whiteflies rise up in a cloud and fly a short distance away.	Handpick and discard infected leaves. Hang yellow sticky traps. Use beneficial insects, including lacewings and parasitic wasps. Wash leaves with soapy water or apply an insecticidal soap, horticultural oil, or hot-pepper spray.

Weevil   Thrips   Mealybugs   Scale   Whiteflies

GREENHOUSE
PROJECTS

You've taken a look at greenhouses inside and out. Maybe you've seen one that's just right for your garden. Or perhaps you've got some ideas, yet you're not sure exactly what kind of greenhouse you need. Whether you decide to build it yourself or have somebody do the work for you, the following pages will help you make some final decisions. You'll find a wide range of greenhouse styles, from simple plastic hoops to fully functioning horticultural houses replete with climate controls.

These designs are more suggestions than strict blueprints—you may end up picking and choosing from several different styles. Perhaps you'd prefer a wood-framed structure, but you'd rather use polycarbonate glazing than glass. You might like the lean-to model, but feel that you need to pour a full concrete foundation. In any case, a full list of greenhouse suppliers is given on pages 110 and 111.

Many of these greenhouses are quite simple to build, but a few are too complex for most home gardeners—they'll require the services of a design firm or general contractor. In all cases, only a qualified electrician should perform electrical installations. For more information about building basics and options, refer back to Chapter 2.

This custom-built greenhouse blends graciously with a stately home (page 108).

PORTABLE PVC

Plastic is the most economical option in do-it-yourself greenhouses. Generally, you build a frame of PVC (polyvinyl chloride) tubing and cover it with some kind of plastic glazing. The quality and durability of these structures vary considerably, and even the simplest model provides just enough extra heat to protect tender seedlings and extend your growing season. The two greenhouses shown here are so lightweight that you can even move them around the garden if need be.

Plastics transmit light and heat to varying degrees. The "hoop house" shown below is covered with plastic film from a greenhouse supplier (page 110). Depending on the type, this film allows in 75 to 80 percent of visible light. To increase the heat retention of plastic film, many gardeners use a double layer of film, installing an air blower to keep the space between the two sheets continuously inflated.

Securing the film to the frame can be difficult, as the fasteners easily tear the plastic. The best solution is to overlay the film at the points of attachment with wood furring strips, aluminum extrusions, or heavy duct tape, then insert fasteners (either nails or staples) through the overlay and the film into the wood beneath.

The gable model shown at right, designed by Farm Wholesale Products of Salem, Oregon, features corrugated polyethylene panels attached to a custom-made PVC frame. Both the frame and the glazing contain UV inhibitors to resist sun degradation and extend the life of the greenhouse. The structure is reinforced with steel tubing in weight-bearing areas—the benches, end walls, and base. Join the panels together with H channels, available from the manufacturer. U trim is used to cap off the open ends. Secure the panels to the framing with self-tapping screws. All joints should be caulked with silicone caulking.

A portable heater is a good substitute when solar heat is lacking, as is a simple heat sink consisting of several large buckets filled with water. Insulation can be further increased in winter by lining the inside of the greenhouse with a layer of plastic bubble wrap.

HOOP HOUSE

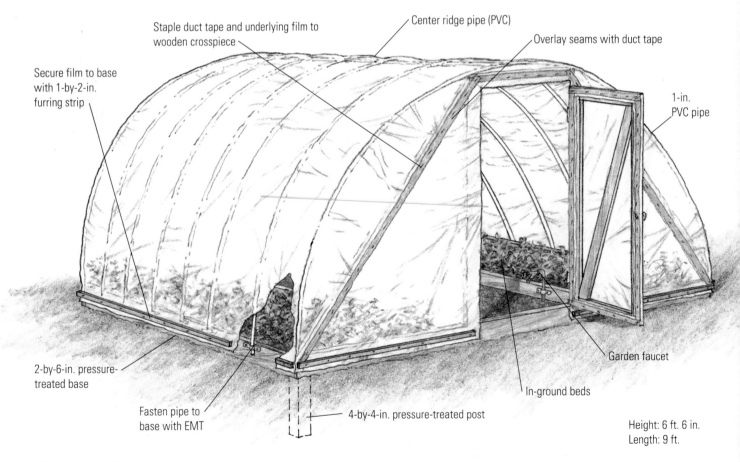

Staple duct tape and underlying film to wooden crosspiece

Center ridge pipe (PVC)

Overlay seams with duct tape

Secure film to base with 1-by-2-in. furring strip

1-in. PVC pipe

2-by-6-in. pressure-treated base

Fasten pipe to base with EMT

4-by-4-in. pressure-treated post

Garden faucet

In-ground beds

Height: 6 ft. 6 in.
Length: 9 ft.

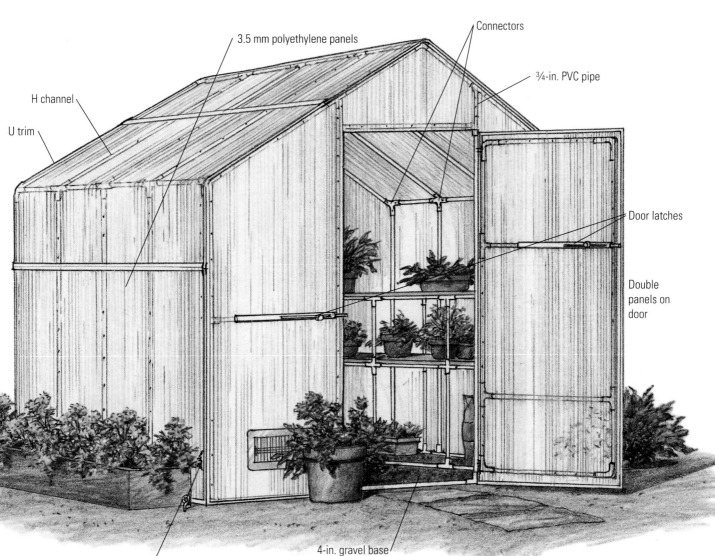

GABLE MODEL

3.5 mm polyethylene panels

Connectors

¾-in. PVC pipe

H channel

U trim

Door latches

Double panels on door

Tie-downs inserted into ground

4-in. gravel base

Height: 9 ft.
Length: 8 ft.

SUNSCREEN FOR GREENHOUSES?

We all know that plants need light for photosynthesis, but why does some greenhouse glazing contain materials to block out certain portions of the light spectrum? Sunlight consists of different wavelengths from ultraviolet (UV) through the familiar colors of the visible spectrum—violet, blue, green, yellow, and red—to infrared. Too much UV light can be harmful to plants, just as it is to humans. And it has a truly destructive effect on plastic glazing, causing it to turn yellow and brittle, and eventually break down. Some materials, such as glass, are naturally UV resistant; others must be coated or impregnated with blocking filters to protect them.

SOLAR PIT

The so-called pit greenhouse takes advantage of the earth's natural insulation properties. Because these models involve relatively little framing and glazing, the materials cost less overall than they do for fully glazed types. However, you'll need more construction expertise, as you must make the structure strong enough to resist pressure from the surrounding earth. The pit greenhouse shown here, which has poured concrete walls, will function efficiently for many years, but you'll have to do a considerable amount of excavation, as well as build concrete forms for the footing and the walls.

Most pit designs require walls that extend about 4 feet underground. You can make the walls of masonry, concrete block, or poured concrete. Then you bolt a treated wood sill to the top of the walls and build up the frame from the sill. For additional heat retention, attach insulated panels to the interior walls.

You can purchase polycarbonate panels from a greenhouse supplier and cut them to fit between the rafters. The most weatherproof method of securing the glazing to the framing is to install aluminum extrusions (also available from a greenhouse supplier) at each point of attachment; in this model, such extrusions hold the glazing to the ridge and rafters. Cut the glazing panels to size, and slot them into channels on the sides of the extrusions (they absorb the glazing's expansion and contraction). Seal the top end of the glazing with aluminum-foil tape. Screw the extrusions to the rafters, and add a bead of silicone caulk down the outside of each channel.

A modified version of this greenhouse would be ideal for a sloping site.

2-by-6-in. ridge

Louver vent

Wooden steps

Height (floor to ridge): 9 ft.
Length: 10 ft.

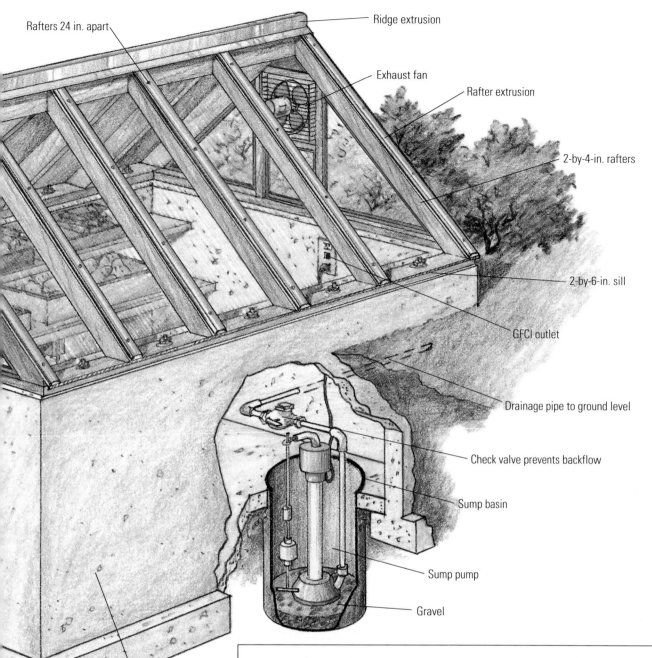

Rafters 24 in. apart

Ridge extrusion

Exhaust fan

Rafter extrusion

2-by-4-in. rafters

2-by-6-in. sill

GFCI outlet

Drainage pipe to ground level

Check valve prevents backflow

Sump basin

Sump pump

Gravel

8-in.-thick poured wall

Poured footing

DRAINAGE

Because they lie below grade, pit greenhouses are subject to flooding. It's essential that you provide sufficient drainage to keep the floor dry. One way to do this is to run 4-inch perforated drainpipe along the outside base of the footing on both long sides of the greenhouse, and cover the pipe with pea gravel.

Another solution is place an electric water, or sump, pump beneath the floor. When pouring the floor, leave a sleeve slightly wider than the top of the pump basin (usually made of plastic or metal). Set the basin into a hole approximately 2 feet below floor level. Fill the bottom of the basin with a few inches of gravel and set the pump into the basin. Plug the pump into a GFCI-protected outlet. Water will flow into the pump pit, activating the pump when it reaches a certain level. The excess water is then pumped out of a drainage pipe to ground level.

WOOD GABLE

If you are handy enough to pour concrete and perform basic carpentry, you can fashion a homemade greenhouse similar to this one, created by Niagara Designs, of Niagara Falls, Ontario. The structure can withstand frozen ground and snow drifts.

The concrete slab shown here is one option for greenhouse foundations. Generally, a concrete-slab foundation should be at least 4 inches thick, with thicker perimeter footings to resist frost heaving, or full concrete footings as shown. You'll need to level the site, then dig down at least 10 inches (or below the frost line) and fill the hole with 6 to 8 inches of gravel or crushed stone. Place a polyethlene moisture barrier on top of the gravel. Then build concrete forms of 2-inch lumber or plywood for the slab pour. Leave sleeves for the drain, as well as for water or electrical lines, if desired. For additional strength, reinforce the slab with rebar every 18 inches.

The roof design calls for overlapping glass joints, a traditional method of glazing that sheds water more easily than butt joints. Set the ⅛-inch tempered-glass sections in glazing compound with pins. The greenhouse is wood framed and plywood sheathed, and has wood roof rafters and collar ties. This design has two sets of window vents; you can achieve greater ventilation by installing louvers or ridge vents.

⅛-in. drainage between bench slats

Use under-bench area for storage

Premanufactured door

Concrete slab 2 to 4 in. above grade

Slope floor to drain at ¼ in. per ft.

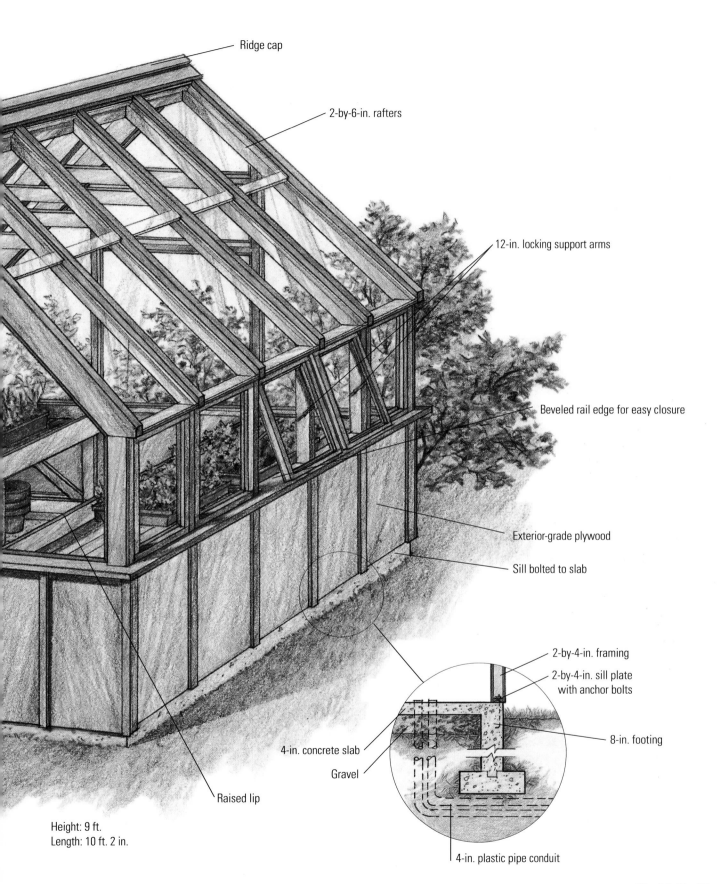

Ridge cap

2-by-6-in. rafters

12-in. locking support arms

Beveled rail edge for easy closure

Exterior-grade plywood

Sill bolted to slab

2-by-4-in. framing

2-by-4-in. sill plate with anchor bolts

8-in. footing

4-in. concrete slab

Gravel

Raised lip

Height: 9 ft.
Length: 10 ft. 2 in.

4-in. plastic pipe conduit

Wood Gable **99**

ALUMINUM-FRAME KIT

Greenhouses built from manufactured kits are an excellent choice for homeowners who have a little construction savvy and a weekend to spare. This one, distributed by Gardenstyles, of Bloomington, Minnesota, consists of an all-aluminum frame fitted with twin-walled polycarbonate panels. It works well for extending your garden's growing season or for growing vegetables and flowers year-round in milder climates.

You need to anchor this fairly lightweight greenhouse to a secure base, such as landscape timbers. Or, as shown here, bolt it to a corrosion-resistant steel base (available from the manufacturer). Sinking base-attached posts into concrete footings gives the structure extra stability. To ensure that the frame is completely square, first assemble the steel base, then dig and pour the footings. Insert the posts and the frame into the wet footings. While the concrete still allows you to move the footings, adjust the frame to make it square and level. Allow the footings to dry, then you can assemble the greenhouse.

Once you've bolted together the frame, secure the panels with nylon gaskets (other models may use spring clips), which fit between the panels and the exterior frame, for a snug fit.

UV-coated polycarbonate

Ridge extrusion

Vinyl-coated shelving

GFCI outlets

Pavers set in sand and gravel

Step

Locking door

Height: 7 ft. 10 in.
Length: 9 ft. 9 in.

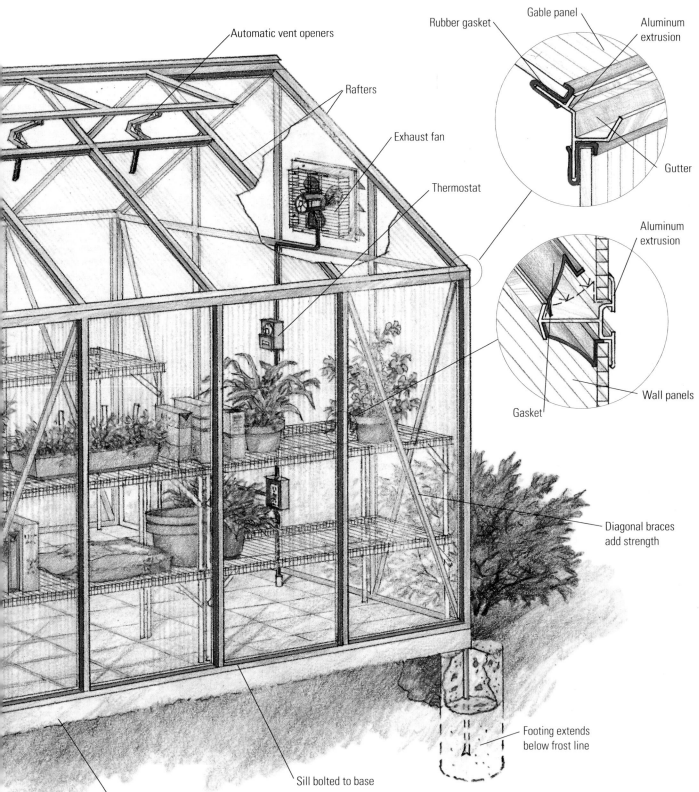

Automatic vent openers

Rafters

Exhaust fan

Thermostat

Rubber gasket

Gable panel

Aluminum extrusion

Gutter

Aluminum extrusion

Gasket

Wall panels

Diagonal braces add strength

Sill bolted to base

Galvanized-steel base

Footing extends below frost line

LIGHTWEIGHT LEAN-TO

Attaching a lean-to greenhouse to an existing house wall saves space in a small garden and costs less than a full-span model. A lean-to also lets you take advantage of GFCI-protected wall outlets and wall faucets to deliver power and water directly into the greenhouse. The wall helps to keep the greenhouse warm and reduces heating costs. This model, from Charley's Greenhouse Supply, in Mount Vernon, Washington, comes with precut twin-walled panels and optional curved eaves of safety glass or acrylic.

For stability, place this greenhouse on a concrete-block or poured-concrete foundation, with or without a poured slab floor. You can bolt it to a raised sill of pressure-treated wood bolted in turn to the concrete with 9-inch anchor bolts (insert these when you're pouring the foundation).

How you attach the greenhouse to the wall depends on your house's siding. For shingled or clapboard walls, you need to make 3 ¾-inch-wide cuts into the shingles to accommodate a 2-by-4-inch mounting frame. For flat siding, stucco, or masonry, bolt a mounting frame directly to the wall, preferably into the house framing members. In all cases, aluminum flashing will protect the siding from water damage. Use glazing tape to seal the polycarbonate panels to the greenhouse frame, and install PVC snap covers to hold the panels to the framing.

Hanging plants secured with brackets

Sliding door

Cedar potting bench with built-in trays

Sill bolted to poured perimeter foundation

Louver vent

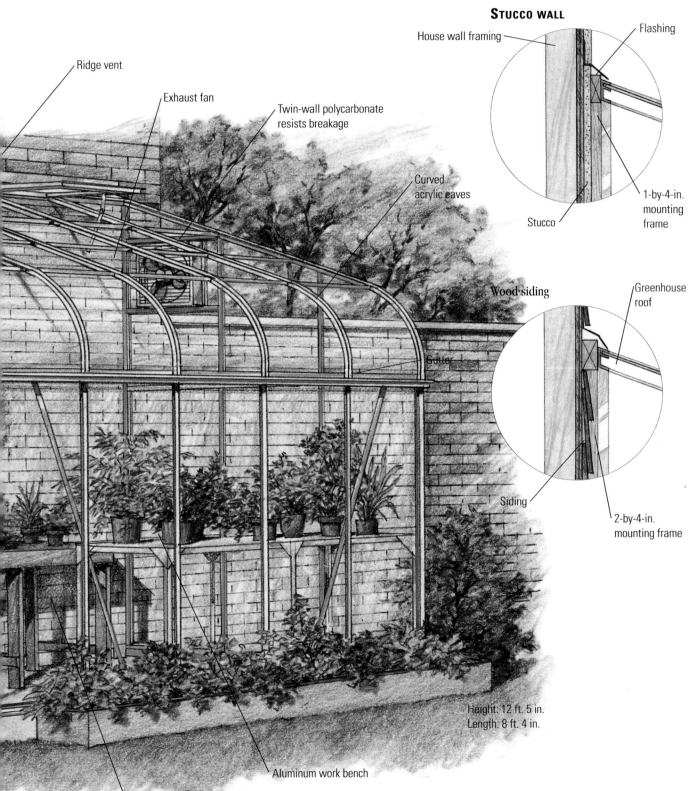

Ridge vent

Exhaust fan

Twin-wall polycarbonate
resists breakage

Curved
acrylic eaves

Gutter

Aluminum work bench

Diagonal braces for strength

STUCCO WALL

House wall framing

Flashing

Stucco

1-by-4-in.
mounting
frame

Wood siding

Greenhouse
roof

Siding

2-by-4-in.
mounting frame

Height: 12 ft. 5 in.
Length: 8 ft. 4 in.

GARDEN-SHED GREENHOUSE

If you don't want a fully glazed greenhouse, but do want a dedicated space for raising seedlings or keeping plants over the winter, consider a structure that is part garden shed and part potting shed. This greenhouse, designed by HDA, of St. Louis, Missouri, is a wood-frame shed with an asphalt-shingled roof and hardboard siding. Windows installed in the roof's long, south-facing slope provide sufficient natural light for growing and propagating plants.

Although this is a substantial structure, it doesn't need a poured foundation—at least not in a frost-free climate. After leveling the site, you dig four trenches 2 inches deep and fill them with gravel. (If your garden has poor drainage, you can make these trenches 6 inches deep.) On top of each trench, place a pressure-treated 4-by-4-inch runner (sometimes called a "skid"). Then lay the floor joists on top of these runners. A wooden ramp sloping up to the door of the shed allows easy passage for a wheelbarrow or lawn mower. The manufacturer suggests Plexiglas for the windows, but you could install glass if you prefer.

You can finish the inside of this shed greenhouse however you like, adding insulation, interior walls, benches, shelves, and of course plumbing and electricity. The beauty of this structure is its versatility—one can easily imagine it serving as a potting shed, a storage room, a workshop, or even a playhouse.

Tri-lap hardboard siding

Potting bench

2-by-6-in. pressure-treated boards for ramp

Height: 11 ft. 3 in.
Length: 10 ft.

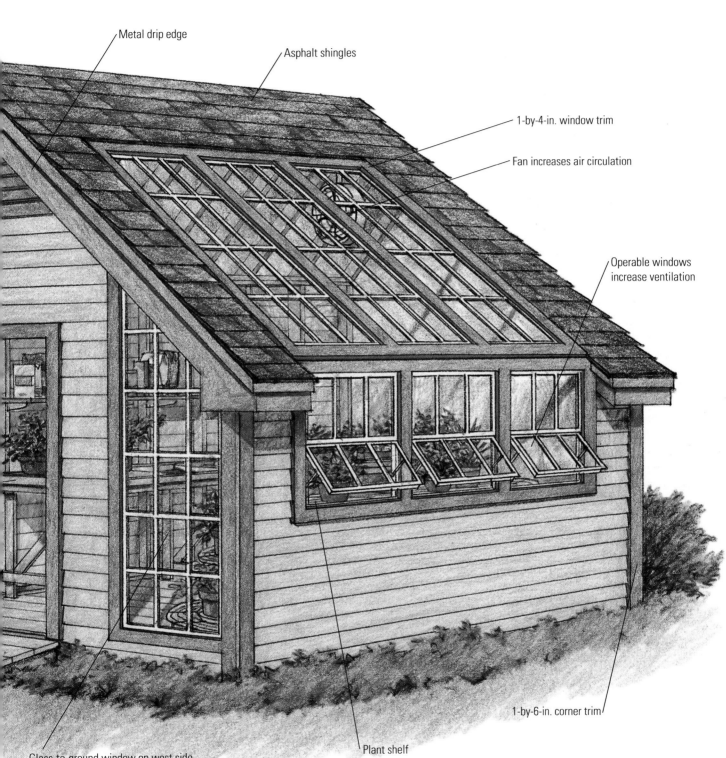

Metal drip edge

Asphalt shingles

1-by-4-in. window trim

Fan increases air circulation

Operable windows increase ventilation

Glass-to-ground window on west side

Plant shelf

1-by-6-in. corner trim

SPACIOUS STAND-ALONE

Designed for use in almost any climate, this large-scale greenhouse was built by the Texas Greenhouse Company, of Fort Worth, Texas. While it offers all the comforts of an English-style horticultural conservatory or greenhouse, the design suits contemporary American gardens well.

Wide enough to accommodate three rows of benches, the greenhouse requires a sturdy poured footing to keep the structure level at all times. Options include an 8-inch-wide raised perimeter footing and a knee wall built as high as 24 inches. The model shown here has glass-to-ground design.

The framing features aluminum glazing bars and a hot-dipped galvanized-steel substructure that is sufficiently strong to support all-glass glazing. This framing has been covered with a white powder coat finish; other colors are available. The roof is either ⅛-inch annealed glass or tempered glass that can withstand hail or falling branches. Put the door openings at floor level, as the floor grade normally lies a few inches above exterior grade. For the interior flooring, use pea gravel, sand, poured concrete or a combination of these; poured concrete calls for an installed drain (page 27).

You can make a greenhouse this size fully climate controlled, with evaporative coolers, automatic vents, heaters, and shading—all operated by control devices that sense temperature, humidity, and light levels. You can also fit this greenhouse with fabric shade cloth or aluminum roll-up lath panels, attached to the outside of the greenhouse.

Full ridge vents

Locking double doors

Freestanding galvanized benches

Length: 20 ft. 5 in.
Height: 10 ft. 6 in.

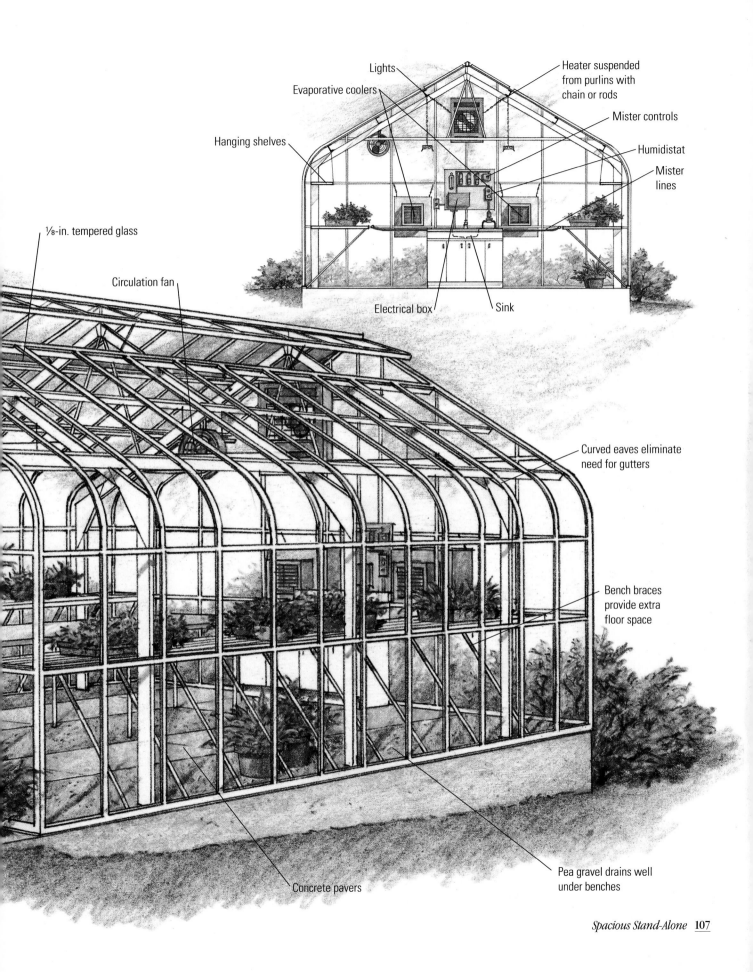

Lights

Evaporative coolers

Heater suspended
from purlins with
chain or rods

Mister controls

Hanging shelves

Humidistat

Mister
lines

Electrical box

Sink

⅛-in. tempered glass

Circulation fan

Curved eaves eliminate
need for gutters

Bench braces
provide extra
floor space

Concrete pavers

Pea gravel drains well
under benches

A CUSTOM JOB

This elegant structure demonstrates how a custom design can integrate a greenhouse with an existing house by using colors that match the house trim and incorporating an existing stone knee wall. This 20-by-12-foot addition is used primarily as a working greenhouse, though the design would also suit a small conservatory.

Rather than relying entirely on the house's heating and cooling systems, the designers have fitted this greenhouse with an evaporative cooler and a heater. A thermostat monitors the interior temperature, opening the ridge vents if it reaches 70°F and turning on the cooler at 75°F. An additional fan circulates air, and gutters on the framing's aluminum extrusions form an internal "weeping" system to reduce condensation. The structure's standard house foundation is 32 inches deep, with a ¾-inch gravel base for the brick-on-sand floor. The aluminum frame has an even-span roof topped with a decorative frieze.

One of the greenhouse walls is an interior house wall, and one is an exterior house wall with a window. This setup offers the advantages of visibility and access from the house. All glazing is tempered glass, and the frame is an attractive bronze color. The structure's outer screen door keeps insects at bay in the summer.

Ridge vents

Thermostat and controls

Inner glass door

Screen door

Sink

Height: 9 ft. 10 in.
Length: 15 ft.

Stone knee wall

Door to house

Track lights

Circulation fan

Clear tempered glass

Window vents

Evaporative cooler

Heater

SUPPLIERS

GREENHOUSE SUPPLIERS

AMDEGA & MACHIN CONSERVATORIES
16 Ostend Avenue
Westport, CT 06880
(800) 922-0110
(203) 368-1675
Red cedar conservatories

ATLAS GREENHOUSE SYSTEMS, INC.
Hwy. 82E, P.O. Box 558
Alapha, GA 31622
(800) 346-9902
fax (912) 532-4600
atlasgrn@surfsouth.com
www.atlasgreenhouse.com
Yard and garden greenhouses specially designed for northern climates

CHARLEY'S GREENHOUSE SUPPLY
17979 State Route 536
Mount Vernon, WA 98273
(800) 322-4707
(800) 233-3078
cgh@charleysgreenhouse.com
www.charleysgreenhouse.com
Greenhouses and full line of accessories

FARM WHOLESALE GREENHOUSE
3740 Brooklake Road NE
Salem, OR 97303
(800) 825-1925
fax (503) 393-3119
www.farmwholesale.com
Greenhouse kits and accessories, corrugated plastic glazing

FOUR SEASONS SUNROOMS
5005 Veterans Memorial Highway
Holbrook, NY 11741
(800) FOUR-SEASONS
fax (631) 563-4010
www.four-seasons-sunrooms.com
Wood and aluminum solariums, patio rooms, and conservatories, do-it-yourself or professional installation

GARDENER'S SUPPLY COMPANY
128 Intervale Road
Burlington, VT 05401
(888) 833-1412
www.gardeners.com
Freestanding and home-attached greenhouses plus accessories

GARDENSTYLES
The Juliana Greenhouse People
10740 Lyndale Avenue, Suite 9W
Bloomington, MN 55420
(800) 203-6409
fax (952) 948-0409
greenhouseexpert@gardenstyles.com
www.gardenstyles.com
European greenhouse kits

GROW-IT GREENHOUSES
17 Wood Street
West Haven, CT 06516
(800) 932-9344
(203) 931-4777
fax (203) 931-4754
info@growitgreenhouses.com
www.growitgreenhouses.com

HOBBY GARDENS GREENHOUSES
P.O. Box 193
New London, NH 03257
(603) 927-4283
fax (603) 927-4292
hgglori@aol.com
www.hobbygardens.com
Greenhouse kits, supplies, and accessories

JANCO GREENHOUSES
9390 Davis Avenue
Laurel, MD 20723-1993
(800) 323-6933
fax (301) 497-9751
info@jancoinc.com
www.jancoinc.com
Greenhouses, solar rooms, and accessories

OAKLEAF CONSERVATORIES
876 Davis Drive
Atlanta, GA 30327
(800) 360-6283
fax (404) 250-6282

PRIVATE GARDEN
Box 600
Hampden, MA 01036
(800) 287-4769
(413) 566-0277
fax (413) 566-8806
dbarry@private-garden.com
www.private-garden.com
Hobby and conservatory greenhouses and accessories

SANTA BARBARA GREENHOUSE
721 Richmond Avenue
Oxnard, CA 93030
(800) 544-5276
fax (805) 483-0229
robsbg@aol.com
www.sbgreenhouse.com
Redwood greenhouses and sunrooms, accessories

SOLAR INNOVATIONS, INC.
234 East Rosebud Road
Myerstown, PA 17067
(800) 618-0669
fax (717) 933-1393
skylight@solarinnovations.com
www.solarinnovations.com

SPECTRUM HOBBY GREENHOUSE CO.
8456 Standustrial
Stanton, CA 90680
(800) 724-2659
spectrumhobby128@aol.com
www.spectrumgreenhouse.com
Greenhouse, sunroom, and solarium kits and accessories

SUNDANCE SUPPLY
Olga, WA
www.sundancesupply.com
Do-it-yourself greenhouses, solariums, and shade houses, polycarbonate materials

TEXAS GREENHOUSE COMPANY
2524 White Settlement Road
Fort Worth, TX 76107
(800) 227-5447
fax (817) 334-0818
tgci@airmail.net
www.texasgreenhouse.com
Greenhouses and cold frames; full line of accessories

TRUELEAF TECHNOLOGIES/ BIOTHERM
P.O. Box 750967
Petaluma, CA 94975
(800) GET-HEAT
(707) 794-9660
fax (707) 794-9663
webmaster@trueleaf.net
www.trueleaf.net
Heating, environmental controls, and irrigation systems

UNDER GLASS MANUFACTURING CORP.
2121 Ulster Avenue
P.O. Box 798
Lake Katrine, NY 12449
(845) 336-5050
fax (845) 336-5097
ugfg@aol.com
www.underglassusa.com
Wide variety of aluminum and glass greenhouses and solariums and accessories

SEED-STARTING SUPPLIERS

A.M. LEONARD, INC.
241 Fox Drive
Piqua, OH 45356
(800) 543-8955
fax (800) 433-0633
www.amleo.com
Free catalog

CHARLEY'S GREENHOUSE SUPPLY
17979 State Route 536
Mount Vernon, WA 98273
(800) 322-4707
(800) 233-3078
cgh@charleysgreenhouse.com
www.charleysgreenhouse.com
Catalog $2

GARDENER'S SUPPLY COMPANY
128 Intervale Road
Burlington, VT 05401
(800) 688-5510
info@gardeners.com
www.gardeners.com
Free catalog

Lee Valley Garden Tools
12 East River Street
Ogdensburg, NY 13669
(800) 871-8158
www.leevalley.com
Free catalog

Seeds of Change
P.O. Box 15700
Santa Fe, NM 87506
(888) 762-7333
fax (888) 329-4762
gardener@seedsofchange.com
www.seedsofchange.com
Free catalog

Southern Exposure Seed Exchange
P.O. Box 460
Mineral, VA 23117
(540) 894-9480
(540) 894-9481
gardens@southernexposure.com
www.southernexposure.com

HYDROPONICS

CropKing, Inc.
5050 Greenwich Road
Seville, OH 44273
(330) 769-2002
www.cropking.com
Hydroponic kits, lights, and more

Dyna-Gro Corp.
1065 Broadway
San Pablo, CA 94806
(800) 396-2476
(510) 233-0254
fax (510) 233-0198
info@dyna-grow.com
www.dyna-grow.com
Hydroponic fertilizers and supplies

Hydrofarm
755 Southpoint Boulevard
Petaluma, CA 94945
(800) 634-9990
fax (707) 765-9977
info@hydrofarm.com
www.hydrofarm.com
Hydroponic supplies and equipment

The Hydroponic Society of America
P.O. Box 2283
El Cerrito, CA 94530
(510) 232-2323
fax (510) 232-2384
www.hsa.hydroponics.org

SPECIALTY PLANTS

Abbey Garden Nurseries
P.O. Box 2249
La Habra, CA 90632-2249
(562) 905-3520
fax (562) 905-3522
Living stones, air plants, cacti, and succulents

Aloha Tropicals
1247 Browning Court
Vista, CA 92083
(760) 941-0920
alohatrop@aol.com
www.alohatropicals.com
Bananas, heliconia, gingers, plumerias, tropical trees, shrubs, and vines

Ann Mann's Orchids
9045 Ron-Den Lane
Windermere, FL 34786-8328
(407) 876-2625
cfog@msn.com
www.cfog.com
Aroids, bromeliads, hoyas, orchids, and supplies

Arid Lands Greenhouses
3560 West Bilby Road
Tucson, AZ 85746
(520) 883-9404
fax (520) 883-8874
Succulents and rare cacti

Exotica Rare Fruit
P.O. Box 160
Vista, CA 92083
(760) 724-9093
fax (760) 940-0914
www.bonusweb.com/exotica
Wide selection of tropical fruit trees

Garden of Delights
14560 S.W. 14th Street
Davie, FL 33325
(800) 741-3103
fax (954)236-4588
godelights@aol.com
www.gardenofdelights.com
Palms, rare fruiting plants and trees

Glasshouse Works
Church Street, P.O. Box 97
Stewart, OH 45778-0097
(800) 837-2142
plants@glasshouseworks.com
www.glasshouseworks.com
Cacti, succulents, and much more

Lychee Woods
721 S.E. Ninth Street
Fort Lauderdale, FL 33316-1209
(954) 728-8089
lychee@safari.net
www.safari.net/~lychee
Tropical and subtropical trees and plants

Stokes Tropicals
4806 E. Old Spanish Trail
Jeanerett, LA 70544
(800) 624-9706
infor@stokestropical.com
www.stokestropicals.com
Bananas, plumeria, gingers, and more

Tropiflora
3530 Tallevast Road
Sarasota, FL 34243
(800) 613-7520
www.tropiflora.com
Bromeliads, tillandsias, orchids, and succulents

ORGANIZATIONS

American Orchid Society
16700 AOS Lane
Delray Beach, FL 33446-4351
(561) 404-2000
(561) 404-2100
theaos@aos.org
www.orchidweb.org
Orchid information and message board

The Cactus & Succulent Society of America, Inc.
2391 E. Cactus Street
Pahrump, NV 89048
(775) 751-1320
fax (775) 751-1357
mpfusaro@pahrump.com
www.cssainc.org

Hobby Greenhouse Association
8 Glen Terrace
Bedford, MA 01730-2048
(781) 275-0377
jhale@world.std.com
www.hobbygreenhouse.org

International Bromeliad Society
Carolyn Schoenau
BSI Membership Secretary
P.O. Box 12981
Gainsville, FL 32604-0981
(352) 372-6589
fax (352) 372-8823
bsi@nersp.nerdc.ufl.edu

Internet Bulletin Boards
http://forums.gardenweb.com/forums
Covers a wide range of plant types and gardening topics

PLANS

HDA, Inc.
4390 Green Ash Drive
St. Louis, MO 63045-1219
(800) 373-2646
fax (314) 770-2226
plans@hdainc.com
www.designamerica.com
Shed plans

Andrew McKechnie, Niagara Designs, Inc.
plans@niagaradesigns.com
www.niagaradesigns.com

INDEX

Page numbers in *italic type* refer to photographs.

Alarms, 38-39
Approvals and permits, 18, 52
Architects, 19, 52
Atrium, *6*
Attached structures, 8, 10
Awnings, 30
Azalea, *57*

Bamboo, *6*
Basements, 22
Beach, *8*
Beds, *45*, 80-81. *See also* Raised beds
  hot, 78
  in-ground, 24, 80, *94*
Begonia, *57*
Botrytis, 89
Boxwood, 9
Bromeliads, 47, 74–75
Brugmansia, 57
Budget, 7
Building codes, 12, 18, 20, 48, 53
Bulbs
  forcing, 73
  propagation, 60, 73

Cactus, 9, 14, 47, 65, 84–85, *85*
Capillary watering, 43, *43*
Climate control, 7, 35, *35*, 48
Cold frames, 78
Conservatories, 10, *47*, 48, *49*
Container gardening, *10, 13, 14*, 56
Containers, 64, *64*, 76, *83*
Contractors, 19, 52
Cooling systems, 35, *35, 107, 109*
Cottage garden, *13*
Cuttings, 22, 60–61, 70–73, 79
Cyclamen, *13*

Damping off, 68, 89
Decking, 8, 12, 27
Dills, Charles, *74*
Diseases, 89
Division, 60
Doors, 7, 30, *30*, 53, *102, 108*
  double, *28, 46, 49, 51, 53, 106*
  hinged, *49, 52, 53, 79, 94, 95, 96, 98, 100, 104–105*
  locking, *29, 95, 100, 106*
Drainage
  depicted, *27, 45, 97, 98*
  discussed, 53, 97, 98, 106
Drip irrigation, 43

Eaves, curved, *48*, 52, *102, 102–103, 106–107*
Electrical connections, 36–37, *37*, 53. *See also* GFCI outlets
Electricians, 19
Ellis, Deborah, *84*
Engineers, 19
Environmental control, *17*, 35, *35*, 48
Equipment and supplies, 64–65

Fall activities, 63

Fans, 7
  depicted, *33, 97, 101, 103, 105, 109*
  discussed, 32, 48, 53
Ferns, 22, *58–59*
Fish, 55
Floor drains
  depicted, *45, 98*
  discussed, 27, 53, 56, 98, 106
Flooring, 26–27, 52
  brick, *9, 26, 52, 58*
  cast iron, *26*
  concrete, *27*, 106
  waterproof, *10*, 50, 53
  wood, *27, 104–105*
Footings
  depicted, *94, 96-97, 99, 101*
  discussed, 25, 96, 98, 100, 106
Foundation, 24–25, 52, 53
Fountains, *54*
Framing, 28–29, 52, 53
  metal, 7, 28, 100–101
  plastic, 29, *94, 94–95, 95*
  wood, 28–29, *29*, 98–99, *98–99*
Fuchsia, *6*
Fungicides, 88
Furnishings, *49*, 50

Garden rooms, 46–57
GFCI outlets, 36, *37*, 53, *97, 100*, 102
Glass, *31*, 52. *See also* Glazing
Glass-to-ground construction, 10, 25, 106, *106–107*
Glazing, *13, 45*, 50, *51*
  acrylic, 102, *103*
  choices, 31, *31*, 52, 53
  glass, 102, 106, *106–107*, 108, *108–109*
  plastic film, 6, *94, 94–95, 95*
  polycarbonate, 31, 96, 100–101, *100–101*
Grapes, *15, 81*
Grow bags, *80*

Hanging plants, 7, 44, *56, 102*
Hardening off, 76
Hardscaping, *12*
Heaters, 22-23, 39, *45, 107, 109*
  bottom, 65, *65*, 66, 78
  choices, 38-39, 53, 67
Herbs, *10, 14*
Humidity, 32, *43*, 50, 53
  automatic system, *14, 42, 107*
  bromeliads, 75
  misting, *15*, 43, 53
  orchids, 67
  plant selection, 9, 56, 57
  water features, *54*, 55
Hydroponics, *82*, 82–83, *83*

Insects
  beneficial, 67
  pests, 67, 77, 85, *88*, 90–91
Insulation, 36, 96
Ivy, *51, 57*

judywhite, *66*

Knee walls
  depicted, 25, *49, 108–109*
  discussed, 25, 44, 52, 108

Landscaping, *11*, 12
Lean-to structures, 10, *11*, 12, 102–103, *102–103*
Lighting, 9, 40–41, *45*, 50
  fish, 55
  lamps, 36, 41
  night lighting, 8, 53
  plant requirements, 47, 56, 57
Lizards, 88
Location, 12, 20–21, 52

Mud rooms, *10*

Nematodes, *88*
Nutrient deficiencies, 87

Orchids, *51, 56*, 65, 66–67
  collection, *6, 10*, 67
  light, *9*, 47
Overwatering, 86

Palms, 56
Paths, *8, 12, 21, 34*
Patios, 12
Peat, 65
Permits, 18, 52
Pesticides, 88, 90–91
Pests, 90–91
Plans, *45*, 92–109
Plant selection, 56–57
Plastic. *See also* Glazing
  film, 31, *31*
  framing, 29, *94, 94–95, 95*
  panels, 31, *31*, 96, 100–101, *100–101*
Plumbing, 19, 42, 52, 55
Ponds, *54*, 54–55
Potting soil, 65
Powdery mildew, 89
Professional assistance, 19
Propagation, *7, 13, 15*, 50, 60–61, 64
  air layering, 70
  bulbs, 73
  cuttings, 70–72, 79
  from seeds, 60–61, 64–65, 68–69
  mat, *35*, 65

Raised beds, *49*, 53, 54, 80
Recycled materials, *30*
Rich, Libby, 22
Rock wool, *83*
Rodents, 86
Roses, *51*
Rust, *89*

Sand, 65, *83*
Sanitation, 85, 88
Seasonal activities, 62–63
Seasonal greenhouses, *6*
Seedlings, 62–63, *68*, 68–69, *69, 76*, 78
Seeds, planting, 60–61, 62–63, 64, 68–69
Shade, 34, *45*. *See also* Lighting
Shade cloth, 7, 34, *34*, 53
Shade-loving plants, 9, 14, 45, 57
Shelving, 44, *45*
Shed, *104–105*
Size, 14, 22-23, 67, 106–107, *106–107*
Skylights, 50, *51*, 52. *See also* Lighting

Soil mixes, 22, *65*
  bromeliads, 75
  cactus and succulents, 85
Soil sterilization, *65*
Solar pit, 96–97
Solarium, 50
Sources, 110–111
Space, using effectively, *45*
Spiders, 88, *88*
Sprayers, *42*
Spring activities, 62
Statuary, *51*
Steps, *96, 100*
Storage, *7, 11, 14, 45*
Style, 6–15
  gable, *94, 95*, 98–99, *98–99*
  garden shed, 104–105, *104–105*
  hoop, 29, 94, **94**
  pit greenhouse, 96–97, *96–97*
  wood cottage, 98–99
Succulents, *6, 51, 56, 85*
  growing conditions, 9, 14, 84–85
  propagation, 72
Summer activities, 62–63
Sump pump, 97
Sunrooms, *11*, 50, *51*

Teepee, *6*
Temperature control, 36, 38, 53, 108, *108–109*
Temperatures, 32, 50, 55, 56–57
Thermal breaks, 28, 52
Thinning, 69
Toads, 88
Tomatoes, *14, 15*
Topiary, 6
Transplanting, 60, 62–63, 76–77
Trees, *11*, 56
Trellises, *45*
Troubleshooting, 86-91

Utilities, 8, 10, 20, 36–37

Vapor barrier, 36
Vegetables, *6, 7, 14, 45*, 81
Vents, 7, 48, 53, 95
  louvered, 30, 32, *32, 33, 96*
  roof, *100–101, 106–107, 108–109*
Vines, *14*
Viruses, 89

Walkways, 45
Water, *45*. *See also* Humidity
  quality, 43, 55, 65
  requirements, 56–57, 67, 75, 85
Water features, 53, 54–55
Water lilies, *54*
Watering, *15*, 42–43, 53, 67
Weather, *8*, 12, 20
Wind, 20, 30
Windows, 30, *30*, 108, *109*
  light, *41*, 50, 104
  operable, 53, *105*
  vented, 7, 98, *98–99*
Winter activities, 62-63

Zoning ordinances, 18